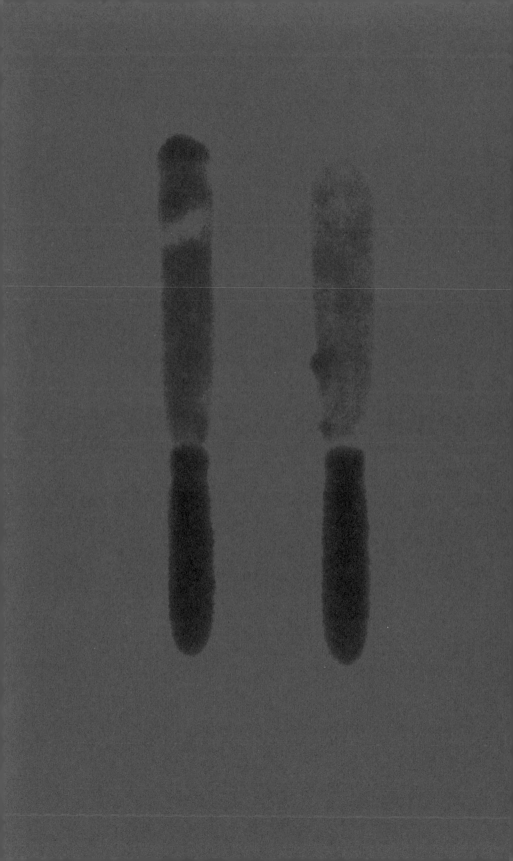

The Shape and Style
of Proust's Novel

John Porter Houston
Indiana University

The Shape and Style of Proust's Novel

Wayne State University Press
Detroit, 1982

Library of Congress Cataloging in Publication Data

Houston, John Porter.
    The shape and style of Proust's novel.

    Includes index.
    1. Proust, Marcel, 1871–1922. A la recherche du temps
perdu. I. Title.
PQ2631.R63A824   843'.912   81–16171
                                  AACR2

Grateful acknowledgment is made for the quotation of "Preludes I," from
Collected Poems 1909–1962 by T. S. Eliot, copyright 1936 by Harcourt Brace
Jovanovich, Inc.; copyright© 1963, 1964 by T. S. Eliot. Reprinted by permission of
Harcourt Brace Jovanovich, Inc., and Faber and Faber Ltd. All quotations from the
French text of Marcel Proust, A la recherche du temps perdu, are by permission
of Editions Gallimard; quotations from the C. K. Scott Moncrieff translation are
from Remembrance of Things Past, Volumes I and II, by Marcel Proust,
translated by C. K. Scott Moncrieff and Frederick Blossom. Copyright 1924, 1925,
1927, 1929, 1930, 1932 and renewed 1952, 1953, 1955, 1957, 1958, 1960 by
Random House, Inc. Reprinted by permission of Random House, Inc.

contents

preface

This book has grown out of over twenty years of teaching and writing about Marcel Proust and fictional technique. The structure of my work observes and then attempts to overcome a dichotomy Proust commented on in his reflections on the narrator's future novel in *Le Temps retrouvé*: there are both truths of the intelligence and epiphanic moments which represent a higher kind of knowledge (3:898–99); all references are to Marcel Proust, *À la recherche du temps perdu*, Bibliothèque de la Pléiade, 3 vols. [Paris: Gallimard, 1954]). In terms of style, these could be epitomized as maxims and images. The former can be rearranged and paraphrased, as I have done, in order to emphasize their interrelations. However, they are also part of the stylistic texture, and style is an absolute manner of seeing things for Proust, a question of vision, and so constitutes the ultimate reality of literature. My argument therefore builds up to a long examination of Proust's verbal art.

My emphasis in chapter 1, which deals with the intellectual armature of Proust's novel, is somewhat different from the usual one. The clichéd version of literary history, however often confuted, holds that Proust's work has something to do with that of Henri Bergson. The reader will find that I make reference rather to German idealism. This was the kind of modern philosophy students in Proust's day became acquainted with in their last year at the lycée and which, if often in a simplistic form, French literary men claimed to espouse. Proust's occasional precise references to Immanuel Kant suggest a more fastidious examination of German philosophy than his contemporaries' allusions often do. (Proust's references to Kant are listed in the name index of volume 3 of his novel and in the name index of Marcel Proust, *Contre Sainte-Beuve précédé de Pastiches et Mélanges et suivi de Essais et Articles*, Bibliothèque de la Pléiade [Paris: Gallimard, 1971].) I believe that the reader will quickly see the relevance for Proust's work of even a second-hand knowledge of the *Critique of Pure Reason* and *The World as Will and Representation*.

For purposes of continuity of language, I have quoted Proust in the C. K. Scott Moncrieff translation in chapters 1 and 2. (The passages in question contain none of the errors which necessitated the recent revision of his work.) However, since there is nothing like a standard edition of this translation, the volume and page references are to the French text. In chapter 3, both the French text and Scott Moncrieff's translation are given, in the hope that students of the modern novel whose French may not be up to reading all of *À la recherche du temps perdu* in the original might be encouraged, with the translation as an aid, to examine some of Proust's characteristic effects in French.

As there are many bibliographies of works on Proust, I have confined myself to references to those works which touch most directly on the questions I treat.

1

the intellectual structure

Categories, Noumena, and Antimonies

Many philosophers, in the wake of Plato, distinguish between two realms—being and becoming, mind and matter, or other such dualisms—in which the philosopher's preference is normally for the half of the antithesis associated with permanence, the "dogmatic" point of view, in Kant's term. *Réalité ordinaire* ("ordinary reality") and *vérité* ("truth") are among the words Marcel Proust uses for his philosophical dichotomy, and he may be indebted to Leconte de Lisle and other French vulgarizers of Indian thought as much as to philosophers like Schopenhauer, whose source is also in part the ancient oriental writings which became known to Europeans toward the beginning of the nineteenth century. A line of Leconte de Lisle's, quoted in *Du côté de chez Swann* as the work of Bergotte, ends a poem titled "La Maya" (in *Poèmes tragiques*, 1884), which we may take as characteristic of one strain of French literary thought when Proust was growing up.

11

Maya! Maya! torrent des mobiles chimères,
Tu fais jaillir du coeur de l'homme universel
Les brèves voluptés et les haines amères,
Le monde obscur des sens et la splendeur du ciel;
Mais qu'est-ce que le coeur des homes éphémères,
O Maya! sinon toi, le mirage immortel?
Les siècles écoulés, les minutes prochaines,
S'abiment dans ton ombre, en un même moment,
Avec nos cris, nos pleurs et le sang de nos veines:
Éclair, rêve sinistre, éternité qui ment,
La Vie antique est faite inépuisablement
Du tourbillon sans fin des apparences vaines.

[Maya! Veil of Appearances! torrent of shifting dreams,
you make spring, from the hearts of all men, brief moments of voluptuous pleasure and bitter hatreds, the dark
world of the senses and the radiant sky; but what is the
heart of ephemeral man, O Maya, but you, the everlasting
mirage? Past ages, coming minutes plunge into your dark-
ness at the same time, along with our cries, tears, and the
blood of our veins: ancient life—a flash of lightning, a sinister
dream, a lying eternity—is unendingly made of the ceaseless
vortex of empty appearances.]

The ideas are related to widespread concerns of romantic literature: the cyclic character of shifting phenomena, the return of all things under the sun and
their opposites, the cessation of desire just as it is to be
satisfied, and the consequent perpetual state of long-
ing for something different and ever-changing. The
force behind the veil of appearances is called Will by
Schopenhauer, and his technical explanation of movement and cyclicity is that a tension arises from the
subject's inability to grasp the object, impelling it
toward still more distant ends. Proust often insists on
the difficulty of enjoying anything present to one's
eyes; self-consciousness hinders true perception of the
object. "When I saw any external object, my awareness that I was seeing it would remain between it and
me, enclosing it in a slender, incorporeal outline which

prevented me from ever coming directly into contact with its materiality" (1:84). Increasing the sense of malaise is the fact that the ego is not content with apprehending the object as phenomenon, but wishes to seize on the thing-in-itself or noumenon, the ultimate, irreducible particularity of the object behind the veil of appearances.

In Proust's ingenious synthesis of idealist philosophy, the noumenon whose existence most impinges on us is the Other, the person whom we by some accident cease to regard as a mere phenomenon and who fills us with the anguish, the sense of incapacity of possession, which is prior rather than subsequent to love in Proust's analysis. At this point the lower and demential form of imagination begins to work, and we invest the other person with another identity completely of our own fabrication. "No doubt very few people understand the purely subjective phenomenon we call love, or how it creates, so to speak, a fresh, a third, a supplementary person, distinct from the person the world knows by the same name, a person most of whose constituent elements are derived from ourself, the lover" (1:468). Jealousy, the basest form of imagination, enters into play, and increases as the impossibility becomes ever more apparent of grasping another's subjectivity (2:158). With his novelistic sense of play, Proust even devises an example of social rather than sexual possessiveness and jealousy, the relation of Mme Verdurin to her clan of faithful (1:189). Finally, the potential resistance of the Other to being possessed manifests itself in hostility of varying degrees of subtleness, and the sense of the Other's essential mystery, a powerful concomitant to the anguish preceding love, is perceived as quasi-demonic. "I should have penetrated, in becoming the friend of one of them—like a cultivated pagan or a meticulous Christian going among barbarians—into a rejuvenating society in which reigned health, indifference to others, sensual pleasures, cruelty, unintellectuality, and joy" (1:830). The reader senses, and his impression is shortly confirmed, that the narrator's reaction to the band of girls in Balbec betrays the most extreme subjectivity and distortion. "If, by chance, I did catch sight of no matter which of the girls, since they all partook of the same special essence, it was as if I had seen projected before my face in a shifting, diabolical hallucination, a little of the unfriendly and yet passionately coveted dream which, but a moment ago, had existed only—where it lay stagnant for all time—in my brain" (1:832). These sinister visions come and go as the narrator's sensual interest in the girls waxes or wanes. The opposite of these visions is not beatitude but indifference.

Schopenhauer observed that poets are fond of claiming life to be a dream: the exterior world is unsubstantial, and nothing proves its existence. Proust is particularly eager, in comparing life and dreams, to establish not so much that the outer world does not exist, but that, in any case, our reality is mental. The point of departure for his philosophy, insofar as it had a personal motivation, might be said to be the fact that while the past clearly does not exist in a material way, memories are very alive and influential upon us; Proust speaks of "the incomprehensible contradiction of memory and nonexistence" (2:769). Since our worlds have a certain degree of order and comparability, mental life must, however, be organized in some fashion, and here Proust draws on Kant's concept of the categories by which we structure experience. Time and space are the initial ones, but after that Proust departs from Kant's quite technical detail and devises more literary categories, such as egotism, intelligence, identity, passion, and habit, as shaping forces (3:896). The "immobility" of our categories and minds, confronted with the chaos of perceptions, marshals them (1:6), and a principle like habit, which Proust frequently invokes, can be both protective, in shutting out disturbing experience, or harmful, by closing us off to new, vital impressions (1:10, 643–44).

Our recognition of other people is an intellectual act, even one of creation.

> We pack the physical outline of the creature we see with all the ideas we have already formed about him, and in the complete picture of him which we compose in our minds those ideas have certainly the principal place. In the end they come to fill out so completely the curve of his cheeks, to follow so exactly the line of his nose, they blend so harmoniously in the sound of his voice, that these seem to be no more than a transparent envelope, so that each time we see the face or hear the voice, it is our own ideas of him which we recognize and to which we listen [1:19].

There is a striking episode in *Le Côté de Guermantes* where the narrator speaks on the telephone to his grandmother and later sees a photograph of her. The telephone, by eliminating our set reactions to a certain face, makes us actually listen to the voice and hear what it is like; the camera functions like an impersonal eye, whose mechanism does not simply supply an image already in us. Finally, there are ideas and preconceptions which do not bear on the body of the person but rather on his whole being, like the appurtenance to a class or "caste," which serves as a sociological category to blind us to others (1:16); our deforming vision, as of national character, may even be dangerous (3:574). Categories tend to create ideas of sameness rather than of particularity, the nature of the thing-in-itself; we derive from them, however, psychological laws—"truths of the intelligence"—of indisputable value (1:899, 515, 892; 2:900).

As we pursue Proust's thought in its relation to Kant's or Schopenhauer's, it becomes apparent that Proust's intellectual constructions do not have the same kind of rigor or detail as the German philosophers'; we must esteem them for their informing value in the novel, as ideas rather than philosophy in a technical sense. This is quite clear when we examine the suspension of the categories, which constitutes an important aspect of Proust's work. Kant was not interested in the momentary cessation of the categories' effects; for Proust, it was as absorbing as their functioning. The opening pages of *À la recherche du temps perdu* are concerned with confusions of time, space, and identity; Proust is trying to suggest that we are never very far from irrational mental states, as our spending one third of our time in sleep readily demonstrates. It is the irrational side of our minds that is basic and primordial.

The most fully described irrational phenomenon is, of course, involuntary memory, and we can consider it to be the highest, the most satisfying form of such experience. Confusions on awakening may be too elemental for us to know we are experiencing them; most dreams are so elusive as to be inaccessible to the pleasures of reflection. With involuntary memory we are able, while still in touch with our ratiocinative faculty, to experience our own consciousness at a point in the past, when we were, of course, other persons than we are now. Involuntary memory is a form of possession of that thing-in-itself which is our earlier existence. The experience of knowing what is actually "another's" subjectivity is so extraordinary as to be called mythical and supernatural (1:48–49), just as the ability to partake of the consciousness of a contemporaneous person would be. In describing it, Proust has recourse to the qualifications "real but not actual, ideal but not abstract" (3:873).

The urge to possess something important yet elusive takes still another form. The contemplation, under favorable circumstances, of certain landscapes may arouse the desire to deepen our experience, as with involuntary memory, to perceive what seems to be hidden behind appearances. The need for effort, for *recherche*, is felt, as in the case of tasting the madeleine and linden tea (1:179). The thing-in-itself which is the landscape—for things are noumena as much as persons—can indeed be intuited, possessed through translation into words, painting, or music. This process is even called "getting rid of it," since in a sense the material object which inspires the work of art vanishes, and only the intangible essence remains. Although Proust does not go so far as to call the landscape an irritant, the demands it makes for its conversion into art are imperious and considerable. The language Proust sometimes uses seems to imply that beauty is hidden in the object, as if there were some sort of concealed message such as one would encounter in a theocentric universe of signs. This merely describes how the summons to create art may appear to one; actually, as Proust is careful to make clear (1:643), truth and beauty are in us, not in the object.

The comparisons Proust makes between music and involuntary memory (3:261) or between landscape impressions and memory (3:878) may at first seem like facile analogies among things he is fond of, but actually his reasoning is tighter. When the narrator thinks of memory as he listens to the Vinteuil septet, he is reflecting on the fact that both express another's subjectivity, the composer's and that of oneself when younger. Furthermore, Proust is principally interested in that stage of understanding a work of art where, after a genuine intellectual effort and the accustoming of the sensibility to something entirely foreign, one first grasps its sense and structure; this is comparable to his description of the effort one must make to penetrate involuntary memories. The narrator, at the time when he makes the analogy, does not yet know that involuntary memory will be a basic part of his esthetic of the novel; he senses that they are somehow linked but does not know how. As for memory and the landscape, again the link is the effort of plumbing, of completely grasping the experience. At the point where the narrator makes the comparison, he has had the experience of writing a prose poem about a landscape, but he is just beginning to see that involuntary memory as well will contribute to his art. These analogies have, in other words, a dramatic function in the narrator's discovery of his vocation.

In the examples of the inability to possess the noumenon and of the attainment of it, I have barely touched on one important relation between subjects and things-in-themselves: when one creates a work of art, the content of one's subjectivity is made accessible to an audience. In this true communication, however, there is no real possession, since the subject-object relation vanishes in esthetic contemplation, as do the deforming effects of the categories. The work of art is not material paint or sounds. In this way, the mode of being of art is like that of involuntary memory, "real but not actual, ideal but not abstract." We should be careful, however, not to assimilate Proust's thought to a Platonic idealism, even though Schopenhauer moved in that direction and Proust uses the word "essence" at times in a way that might imply realities *ante rem* and *supra rem*. Proust does not want to suggest the generalizing character of the Platonic idea, for art is the world in which the irreducible individuality of the mind is revealed, and ordinary experience, through its subjective color, becomes precious (1:720). Proust calls it the world of differences, in distinction to that of generalities, which express common traits, and it is these differences which constitute the highest truth and the condition of beauty. It is obvious that an esthetic based on such thinking will differ sharply from a neoclassical, universalizing one, but, at the same time, Proust does not completely discard the wisdom of maxims and typologies.

There is a domain of lower truths for Proust, and the expression "psychological laws" is the general term for it, although much of its content refers to historical change and sociological configurations. These truths of the intelligence are not absolute like the truth of beauty, which is perceived by the imagination, yet they have a genuine function not only in life but in literature as well. Proust sees the novel as made up of two kinds of material, the more precious being the apprehensions of beauty, the lesser consisting of general laws; translating this into terms of Proust's style, we might say they correspond to images and maxims.

We can observe that the power of persuasion of art and beauty is always greater than that of intelligence, so that when we attempt to think about historical periods, it is the artifacts of the past that determine our conceptions. They express not only the artist's or craftsman's subjectivity, but a kind of collective one as well. The artist's selection of subject will constitute the truth of his age, just as Renoir's portrait of Mme Charpentier, the wife of the naturalists' publisher, will establish her as the late nineteenth century's ideal of elegance for all future times, rather than some duchess of Guermantes of the day. This effect of art operates on us in respect to the present as well: his contemporaries always found that women looked like Renoir's portraits, never the inverse. The fact that we know Mme Charpentier's salon was not more elegant than others or that Renoir used models is perfectly idle; we instinctively believe art is the truth of history or the visual, and only with a certain effort can we dissociate them and reduce art to an idiosyncratic or merely imitative role.

The faculty by which we apprehend art is the imagination, but it can function on a lower level as well: jealousy is the result of its turning toward another person as if to a work of art. This symmetry is basic to Proust's thought. Both art and certain other people fascinate us by the mystery of subjectivity; the work of art gradually reveals to us the artist's consciousness, but we can never grasp another person's inner life. Vain attempts to do so, complicated by sexual desires which have their origin in the feeling of mystery, irritate the will to possess, which finds its expression in jealousy. The work of art, which is not an object since it is real but not actual, offers the only true cessation of the will. Because there is a sharp division between the satisfying higher imagination, which properly focuses on art, and the often frustrating lower imagination, which exercises itself in life, one cannot pretend that life can be a work of art, as in Walter Pater's idea of turning one's existence into a thing of beauty and burning with a hard gemlike flame. A particular case of this shallow kind of estheticism lies in Swann's mania for imagining that people look like paintings; his wretched love for Odette derives in part from his notion that she resembles a Botticelli.

The imagination can entertain certain elements of life, providing it does so in solitude and away from the side of life it is seeking to isolate and understand. "This dim freshness of my room was to the broad daylight of the street what the shadow is to the sunbeam, that is to say, equally luminous, and presented to my imagination the entire panorama of summer, which my senses, if I had been out walking, could have tasted and enjoyed in fragments only" (1:83). Or we can see the differences between individuals better if they are not present and talking (3:954). This freedom for reflection and for true perception comes about, of course, because of the suppression of the subject-object relationship and its tensions. Certain graces of life, fashion, "the Arts of Nothingness," as Proust terms the skills necessary to create salons or individuals such as Saint-Loup—molded by generations of noble customs and almost comparable to artifacts—suggest that analogues of art can exist in the lower realm of appearances and cyclicity.

> Perhaps that special class of society which included in those days women like Lady Israels, who mixed with the women of the aristocracy, and Mme Swann, who was to get to know them later on, that intermediate class, inferior to the Faubourg Saint-Germain, since it ran after the denizens of that quarter, but superior to everything that was not of the Faubourg Saint-Germain, possessing this peculiarity that, while already detached from the world of the merely rich, it was riches still that it represented, but riches that had been canalized, serving a purpose, swayed by an idea that was artistic, malleable gold, chased with a poetic design, taught to smile; perhaps that class—in the same form, at least, and with the same charm—exists no longer [1:639].

At the same time, "the beauty of life" is a meaningless phrase (1:852); the pseudo artists like Swann and Charlus, who seek novelistic situations in reality and compare people with paintings, are not altogether superior to the ignoramuses they despise, and the refinement of their existences simply points the way to more empty *social life*. Nevertheless, it would be mistaken not to understand that some idea of art, however debased, is behind them, and that even snobs, with their false ideal, are following a vulgar parody of taste and esthetic distinctions.

Proust drew attention to "the kind of relief you feel in Kant when, after the most rigorous demonstration of determinism, you discover that above the world of necessity, there is the one of freedom" (2:477). The two worlds can be seen as primarily antithetical in regard to large metaphysical concepts. The simultaneous truth, in different domains, of opposing laws forms the series of Kant's antinomies, like the dual existence of determinism, in the perspective of empirical evidence, and of freedom, according to dogmatic philosophy. Proust's thought contains a number of such antithetical and complementary truths: science shows we are alike, but art shows we are irreducibly individual; psychological laws govern our behavior, but we are composed of a series of discontinuous, irregular mental events; the past is nothingness, but memory of the past influences us; truth consists of general statements, but truth also lies only in the revelation of particulars. Much of the cogency and complexity of Proust's novel comes from the antinomial laws informing it, which are not always directly stated, least of all in the form of an antinomy. Of them, one that underlies the whole unfolding of Proust's novel, and implies Kant's theme of freedom and determination, pertains to the narrator's psychological life.

Correspondences between the Higher and Lower Realms in Proust's Thought

Higher	*Lower*
Art or true life	Ordinary life or reality
Noumena	Phenomena
Truth of beauty and philosophy	Historical and psychological laws
Art as the world of differences	Science as the world of similarities and generalities
Freedom	Determinism
Involuntary memory	Voluntary memory
Art as subjectivity	Art as technique, mimesis, or observation
Style as imagery	Style as maxims
Formal art	The Arts of Nothingness or the elegant enhancement of life
Mystery of mythic qualities	Demythification into ordinary reality
Imagination as the grasp of another's subjectivity through art	Imagination as the vain pursuit, through jealousy, of another's subjectivity
Alluring mystery of the Other	Unpleasant sexual secret of the Other

Fall, Will, and Redemption

As the narrator of *À la recherche du temps perdu* begins to tell of the "drama of my going to bed" in Combray, he evokes images of persecution: Geneviève de Brabant and Golo, who make him think of his mother and of his grandmother's anguish over her husband's being given cognac purposely to upset her. The narrator is filled with moral anguish and scruples over such cruelty, and shortly thereafter, as the specific evening of Swann's coming to dinner is recounted, he himself will be the victim of his father and grandfather, who do not obey the rules of treaties and send him to bed early, "without the last sacrament." Proust continues with metaphors and comparisons suggestive of barbaric laws, abrupt condemnations even to death, and savage religious exigencies. To take one example, the father looks, as he ascends the stairs later, like Abraham going to sacrifice Isaac. In this atmosphere saturated with arbitrary ferociousness, the narrator has a fantasy of his mother in the "forbidden," "hostile" dining room, in the "inconceivable," "infernal" rites, where amid "unknown," "malefic" pleasures and "inimical, perverse, and exquisite" throngs she "laughs" at him. This demonic imagery is explained as a consequence of his "anguish," a free-floating emotion which, before adult sexuality enters his life, can be directed toward a parent or friend. In other words, this anguish, with the visions it brings, is a primal given fact of his sensibility; it does not derive from any anterior experience. It arises, of course, from the frustrated will to possess the Other. A similarly demonic vocabulary is used later not only for Mlle Vinteuil's erotic practices and for Odette's hidden private life, but also for Gilberte's ultimate, taciturn hostility, for the frieze of girls against the sea in Balbec, and above all for the later experiences with Albertine, who the narrator fears will "laugh at him while doing evil" (3:21). In Swann's case, such jealous fantasies enter only with his attachment to Odette, but for the narrator there is hardly any emotional configuration more innate.

The conflict of great forces can be implied in the French word *drame*, which often suggests something of what English speakers would call "melodrama." The evening does not end with the narrator's death or expulsion from the family, as he fears, despite the fact that he commits the worst offense in the "hierarchy of sins," which is to give in to a "nervous impulse" because of his original anguish. The mother, after trying to hide him from the father, as if he were a clandestine lover ("Run, run, don't let your father catch you there"), is urged by her husband to spend the night with the child. This is against the mother and grand-mother's principle of not yielding to the child's emotions, in order to "fortify his will"; the night spent with his mother is remembered as a major event in his life, a "puberty of tears," after which his nervousness will be regarded as an involuntary affliction rather than a sin. Perhaps, however, it would be better to explain the child's condition as a perversion of will: his nervous impulses represent willing evil and not good. It is not only to fortify but also to direct his will that the mother and grandmother have erected their hierarchy of sins. In any case, the whole moral theology of the child's life is overthrown; his will is recognized as irremediably weak or self-indulgent, and his failing flesh will no longer be punished. This compromise with evil profoundly upsets the narrator, and a new kind of remorse enters his life; his fantasies now are of his mother aging in sorrow over her defeat. In other words, time enters the world with the fall, and her death is to be a far greater punishment for the narrator than the ones he had previously suffered for his sins of will. She has abdicated, and, interestingly enough, the narrator notes that the decline in his health dates from that moment (3:886–87). This "sweetest and saddest evening" of his life fills his thoughts at the end of the novel, when he is about to redeem past time through, among other things, a great effort of will (3:886, 1044).

In the meantime, the narrator suffers considerably from the "disastrous way" our "psychopathological mechanism" works (3:457). Irrational feelings of guilt toward his parents are always ready to flare up. He imagines that if they could be brought to see the

Swanns in the enchanting light he does, he would be "wretched, as if I had conquered and depraved them" (1:144). When he persuades his parents to allow him to go to the theater, he ceases really to wish to, because "their consent made me love them so, that the idea of giving them sorrow caused me to feel it myself" (1:443). Indeed, the whole theater episode is treated as if the performance of *Phèdre* were an object of perverted desire, to remind the parents of original sin and fall. This becomes explicit when the narrator meets Bergotte, which "appeared to them as a disastrous but natural consequence of a first sin, of the weakness they had had" (1:573). The grandmother's general behavior is in the same vein. It is hardly surprising that the narrator begins to show a general neurotic inability to behave in a way best suited to furahering what he wishes. His first attempt to meet Albertine is characteristic: as he sees Elstir talking to Albertine and her friends on the beach, he suddenly feels that, since the introduction is now made so easy and immediate, he need not hurry to take advantage of it. As we move to satisfy a desire, we are modified by that movement, so that the desire is no longer the same in the economy of our emotions; desire therefore cannot be truly satisfied (3:575–77). Of course, as soon as Albertine leaves, unmet, he regrets it (1:856). In the initial, archetypal scene in *À la recherche*, the object of perverted will, once attained, ceases to content the narrator. From this derive all the volitional paradoxes of the novel.

Rather near the beginning of the long central Albertine narrative, running from *Sodome et Gomorrhe* II-2 through *La Prisonnière*, there is a reenactment of the bedtime drama. The narrator sends a servant to fetch Albertine to console him; she does not come (2:797). Key words from the Combray episode dominate the account of the narrator's relations with Albertine at this period: *calme* and *angoisse/anxiété* (e.g., 2:1017–19). (They had already served for Swann and Odette.) In other words, only his nervous impulses and the relieving of them now preoccupy the narrator; the basic difference between his love of Gilberte and his obsession with Albertine lies in his further, progressive atrophy of volition (1:586). By this point we see another distinction as well in his drama of the will. In desiring the objects of weakness or perverted will, the narrator is subjected to matter and the determinism it always implies, for the possession of the Other expresses itself in him as physical domination. It is clear in *La Prisonnière* that such material enslavement brings no surcease of the will to possess, however, and even ends with the subjugation of the possessor. The object of right will appears by contrast to be detached from matter and compatible with freedom. Determinism and liberty in Proust have strong analogies with the elaboration of those concepts in Christian theology.

There is a great drawing together of themes at the end of *Sodome*. The image of Vinteuil's daughter and her lesbian practices at Montjouvain, which was isolated, unconnected in "Combray," as it was also in the narrator's memories, finally recurs.

> At the sound of these words, uttered as we were entering the station of Parville, so far from Combray and Montjouvain, so long after the death of Vinteuil, an image stirred in my heart, an image which I had kept in reserve for so many years that even if I had been able to guess, when I stored it up long ago, that it had a noxious power, I should have supposed that in the course of time it had entirely lost it; preserved alive in the depths of my being—like Orestes, whose death the gods had prevented in order that on the appointed day, he might return to his native land to punish the murderer of Agamemnon—as a punishment, as retribution (who can

tell?) for my having allowed my grandmother to die, perhaps; rising up suddenly from the black night in which it seemed forever buried, and striking, like an Avenger, in order to inaugurate for me a novel, terrible, and merited existence, perhaps also to make dazzlingly clear to my eyes the fatal consequences which evil actions indefinitely engender [2:1114–15].

The narrator's killing his grandmother is a totally irrational fantasy; he is constructing a moral theology in which all events can be referred to a system of original sin and its indefinite propagation of crime. The *Oresteia* is one of the most striking embodiments of such a system, and the reference serves to suggest to us a highly theologized vision of the world without exclusively Christian associations.

The death of the parents (the grandmother is a frequent substitute for the mother in the novel) is, of course, in the Freudian myth the deserved consequence of incest, the desire for which seems implicit in the jealousy imagery in the *drame du coucher*. The latter recurs as the narrator thinks of Albertine's earlier years in Trieste.

It was Trieste, it was that unknown world in which I could feel that Albertine took delight, in which were her memories, her friendships, her childish loves, that exhaled that hostile, inexplicable atmosphere, like the atmosphere that used to float up to my bedroom at Combray, from the dining room in which I could hear Mama talking and laughing with strangers, amid the clatter of knives and forks, Mama, who would not be coming upstairs to say goodnight to me; like the atmosphere that had filled for Swann the houses to which Odette went at night in search of inconceivable joys. It was no longer as of a delicious place in which the people were pensive, the sunsets golden, the church bells melancholy, that I thought now of Trieste, but as of an accursed city which I should have liked to see go up in flames and to eliminate from the world of real things [2:1121].

Here we have one of the best examples of the way the *drame du coucher* functions as archetypal situation and source for the narrator's emotions in adult life, and of the prefiguring role Swann's liaison with Odette plays. Again, we see the material character of the determinism governing him. He cannot deal with his anguish because it is embodied in concrete persons and things, which it is beyond his power to control.

In *La Prisonnière*, although the narrator admits it is sacrilege, he sees Albertine's kiss as his mother's (3:10); in fact, with his age and weakened will, Albertine becomes sister, daughter, and mother to him (3:11). This suggests the promised chapter on mothers profaned (2:908) and reminds us the father is profaned in the Montjouvain episode. Theologically the narrator is lost to good, subsisting solely on the negation of his affliction, calm or indifference succeding anguish. After Albertine's departure, a new word, "hell," enters his vocabulary, as actual knowledge of Albertine's past replaces the fantasies of anguish and jealousy. Hell is the realization of the immobile concreteness of past deeds, which a change of mood cannot alter, as it can what is only suspected or imagined.

The idea of resurrection subtly underlies the language of the madeleine episode in *Swann*, following directly on the *drame du coucher*, with its implications of time and death. "Dead forever?" are the words introducing the madeleine scene, and the metaphors are of memory *rising*. We have there, at the beginning, in miniature, and with little underscoring, the larger pattern of the novel: after the fall and long decadence of powers comes renewal; the narrator feels free from time and contingency as he tastes the madeleine. The idea of art as the artist's immortality occurs in the episode of the death of Bergotte, where we also find the notion that though there may be no other world, we live as if one existed (3:188). Reparation for time lost, for the "double assassination" of the grand- mother and Albertine, introduces the idea of moral salvation, which pervades the meditation on art to- ward the end. The narrator is about to affirm his childhood values by a creative act of will, and the spell cast over him by his mother's abdication will be dissipated. Art and moral values together represent the highest and most powerful immaterial entities, and they are the proper objects of will; lower ones are perverse and enslave their seeker to never-ending determinism, so that will leads paradoxically to its own destruction.

The identification of the work of art with moral values, which becomes entirely clear only at the end of *À la recherche*, brings together the strains of idealist philosophy of knowledge and ethical voluntarism which have been present since the beginning. There is a correspondence between the higher and lower levels of imagination (perception of an artist's subjectivity through art and the vain attempt through jealousy to capture the lover's subjectivity) and the higher and lower levels of the ethical realm (the right object of will and the perverted misdirection of that faculty). The derivation of Proust's epistemology from idealism is readily traceable, particularly since Proust made sev- eral quite precise references to Kant in *À la recherche* and elsewhere, but his moral philosophy has a less Kantian quality. Its Catholic coloring reflects Proust's religious education, and its para-Freudian aspects ob- viously spring from the same late nineteenth-century culture that contributed to the theories of psycho- analysis. (While other sides of Freud's thought were known in France before World War I, the notion of the Oedipus complex was not, so that direct influence seems out of the question.) Although for purposes of analysis we are justified in separating the Kantian idealist, the Catholic voluntarist, and the para-Freudian strains in Proust's thinking, the more impressive fact, however, is not the influences but the harmonious synthesis of them. Proust was, of course, almost forty years old when he began *À la recherche*; he had read and written a great deal since late adolescence, and all rough edges in his system of ideas had been smoothed out in the process of applying it in his various published and unpublished works. This lengthy preparation—comparable to the time Balzac spent experimenting before *Le Père Goriot* or Flaubert before *Madame Bovary*—assured Proust of that kind of homogeneity in the realm of ideas he was obsessed with in the domain of style.

One further aspect of Proust's thought and sensibility remains to be explored here: myth as a way of perceiving and thinking. Again, the effort toward wholeness and homogeneity is apparent in Proust's working out of his themes. Mythic places and relations represent an outpouring of the imagination in early years, when one is too young to create art and to realize the discreteness of art and life, and when the relative greatness of works of literature and music in relation to one another is not yet distinguished. This transformation of life through imagination encompasses the domains of the higher and lower imaginations, putting elegance in living, masterpieces of painting, and negligible pieces of fiction all on the same plane. It is not a perversion of sensibility, being natural and appropriate to one's apprentice years, and the confusions and disappointments it leads to are essentially anodyne. Ultimately the work of art of a lifetime will benefit from these youthful confusions as much as from the imaginative vistas which produced them.

Myth, Experience, and Values

Proust's youthful narrator not only has a myth, as we shall see, but also generally perceives the world in a mythic fashion. Certain names, places, persons, and moments, such as January 1, are infused with an intense quality of value and significance which can only be called "supernatural," in the strict sense of the word. This leads to curious causes and relations: he is at the age when "you think you create what you name" (1:91); "I did not separate people and landscapes" (1:157); the last syllable of "Guermantes" has an orange sound, in keeping with the nineteenth-century myth of synesthesia; centuries of history are perceptible in the figure of a Guermantes. The general word in Proust for the special mythic value is *mystère* ("mystery"), and it is found most of all in everything pertaining to the two ways at Combray, which lead from the real village toward unreachable, archetypal goals: to the content of certain books, which seem to be something other than mere fiction and to represent the ultimate reality; to the Swanns' life in Paris; to Mme de Guermantes, and, for a time, to the girls in Balbec. All of these conceal something, appear to the narrator not as profane, dead, or indifferent phenomena, but as life-giving things-in-themselves, which must be penetrated—and here we perceive the philosophical and intellectualizing bias which separates Proust's novel from a naive representation and acceptance of myth. Because something must be done with things-in-themselves, their sacred, nourishing quality understood, the mythic always points toward the future in Proust.

Paradoxically, the future holds in store something other than revitalizing oneself at the mythic sources;

the sense that life contains two categories, the super-natural and the merely phenomenal, gradually vanishes. Demythification takes place when familiarity erodes the sense of mystery, as when the Swanns' apartment and conversation begin to seem less than enchanted, but this does not mean that all interest evaporates from what ceases to have mythic value. The narrator goes on to perceive such sociological facts as the new class represented by Odette, with its money, elegant taste, and anglomania. The wonderful final image of Odette by the Étoile around one o'clock, on a sunny day in May, shows us the important truth that what has lost the supreme quality of the highest, most mysterious poetry can still have a lower order of esthetic value which is far from negligible. "And as the average span of life, the relative longevity of our memories of poetical sensations is much greater than that of our memories of what the heart has suffered, long after the sorrows that I once felt on Gilberte's account have faded and vanished, there has survived them the pleasure that I still derive—whenever I close my eyes and read, as it were, upon the face of a sundial, the minutes that are recorded between a quarter past twelve and one o'clock in the month of May—from seeing myself once again strolling and talking thus with Mme Swann beneath her parasol, as though in the colored shade of a wisteria bower" (1:641). We hear in this passage another voice speaking than that of the young narrator. This mature voice, whom the tenses do not always betray so clearly as here, knows that the higher realm of art has analogues in the lower world of appearances; he is content with less than the perception of the mythic. In this connection we must note a general technical feature of the early parts of *À la recherche*.

The mythic mode of perception tends to lead us into dense imagistic representations, of the kind "Combray" is especially rich in.

> Nor could we ever reach that other goal, to which I longed so much to attain, Guermantes itself. I knew that it was the residence of its owners, the Duke and Duchess of Guermantes; I knew that they were real people who did actually exist, but whenever I thought about them, I pictured them to myself either in tapestry, like the "Coronation of Esther" which hung in our church, or else in changing, rainbow colors, like Gilbert the Bad in his window, where he passed from cabbage green, when I was dipping my fingers in the holy water fount, to plum blue when I had reached our row of chairs, or again altogether impalpable, like the image of Geneviève of Brabant, ancestress of the Guermantes family, which the magic lantern sent wandering over the curtains of my room or flung aloft upon the ceiling—in short, always wrapped in the mystery of the Merovingian age, and bathed, as in a sunset, in the orange light which glowed from the resounding syllable "antes" [1:171].

These extraordinary stylistic resources are not used in the manner of a merely descriptive writer like Théophile Gautier (whose style Proust disdained), but rather to convey a spiritual state of which the perception of color is merely one aspect. Such epiphanic moments are hardly compatible with recounting actions, however. Since the reader would be dazed at the presentation of the narrator's early life solely from his mythic point of view, we hear two narrating voices: a young one telling of the fullness of his experience, and an older one commenting, sometimes ironically, on the younger one's distortion of what common sense calls reality. (For a more elaborate interpretation see Marcel Muller, *Les Voix narrative dans "À la recherche du temps perdu"* [Geneva: Drox, 1965].) We feel this double level of narration quite strongly toward the end of the reception at Mme de Villeparisis's, which is the last event of the stage of living by myth. "I was delighted with Mme de Guermantes, Saint-Loup, Mme de Marsantes, M. de Charlus, Mme de Villeparisis," says the enraptured narrator, after his older voice has told us the nastiest things about these people (2:283).

The living by myth to which I have alluded is not entirely the same thing as mythic perceptions, but pertains to that part of the thematic movement of *À la recherche* which one might term "the quest." There is indeed a quest in *À la recherche*, which can be distinguished somewhat from the "plot": the young narrator is engaged in finding the secret of truth and beauty (1:84). Beauty he perceives much of, but its truth, its mode of being, is not yet apparent to him. The particular myth which governs his quest is the identity of future experience with imaginative life, and the pursuit of Gilberte, who clearly represents truth, beauty, and mystery, both in herself and as the friend of Bergotte, is the first active, concrete manifestation of the narrator's living by his myth. But, as we have seen, the tendency of myth to draw us constantly toward further absorption into its timeless essence is counterbalanced by the profane, temporal movement of experience.

In the large-scale organization of *À la recherche*, that stage of the narrator's life lasting until the death of his grandmother is conceived of as a time of innocence as opposed to experience, of a lingering faith in his myth. It is marked by his love for Gilberte, Albertine, and Mme de Guermantes, but there is another significant theme also related to myth, and that is the narrator's vocation. Since art for him is above all mythic beings in sympathetic landscapes, its creation cannot result merely from an ordinary act. Indeed, the narrator, who has heard many commonplaces about writers, has tried to sit at a desk and think of an idea, but such attempts are incommensurate with the nature of art, and he has had to resort to the mythic hypothesis of a magic deed on the part of his father which will bring about his transformation into a writer. The only alternative is to suppose there is no mystery in his future, no truth beyond ordinary reality (1:173). The naive character of these reflections should not hide the fact that they resemble the mature narrator's hypothesis that if art is merely a technique of imitating life, then it has no value. Since every artist's oeuvre is individual and unpredictable, the young narrator makes no connection between his received ideas on how writers invent art through intelligence, which he is sure he does not possess, and his own most intimate ideal, which is to know Mme de Guermantes amid the red and violet flowers of her garden and frequently to smell the odor of the toilets in the Champs-Élysées, which evoke Combray (1:569). He has the greatest difficulties accepting set ideas about the good, the true, and the beautiful, and disgusts his grandmother, who would like him to have long, edifying, and inspiring conversations about art with Elstir, instead of wasting his time with Albertine and her friends. High seriousness is lost on the narrator, and he observes what pleasure he has in being silent with the *jeunes filles en fleurs*, rather than in discussing ideas and the important events of past and present with Mme de Villeparisis or Robert de Saint-Loup. There is an irony in the *temps perdu* or "time wasted" of Proust's title for his novel. For the high-minded, the narrator has indeed wasted his time pursuing mythic values in the vulgar Swanns or in the smell of a toilet.

Two important events occur in the middle of *Le Côté de Guermantes*: the race of Combray dies, in the person of the grandmother; and the last of the narrator's youthful loves, that for Mme de Guermantes, fades away–although, in Proust's characteristic indirect narrative method, we do not learn immediately about the latter. The race of Combray (Proust is fond of mythical races) does not, of course, literally die with the grandmother, for the mother still lives and reincarnates her, but the phase of the novel concerned with the myths of childhood and adolescence and with the straightforward opinions about people and things held by the traditional village comes to an end with her death. Much later, the narrator and his mother remark that it is better she be dead than see the upheavals in the caste system which have taken place (3:658). The grandmother is narrow-minded in her way, and certainly incapable of perceiving the highest manifestations of art; she is not intended to seem perfect. Rather, it is an ingenuous notion of good and of beauty which she stands for, and which is essentially that of the narrator when he speaks, up to this point, in his younger or naive voice.

Almost from the beginning of *Guermantes* II-2 we sense a difference in the narrator; it is finally made explicit during the dinner party at the house of the duchess of Guermantes. He is over his infatuation; he is also over a complete denigration of the Guermantes and can see the "little drop of originality" which makes them minor art works in the dull world of society. The disparity between a naive narrating voice and a disillusioned one no longer exists. The Guermantes and their friends, descended from myth to esthetic objects, fulfill the narrator's hopeful expectations when some talk genealogies and make little pretense of being like other people. In this new phase of experience and measured judgment, much pleasure is to be found in such local color, and the mythic is no longer sought after. But there is a further shade of experience. At the end of *Guermantes* II, when Swann pays a call on the duke and duchess at the same time as the narrator, they refuse to listen to Swann's explanations that he is fatally ill; they rush off to a dinner party because the duke is *dying* of hunger and the duchess *dead* from fatigue. They also manage to say a good deal about ancestors and avoid a servant's reminder that a cousin of theirs will not last the night. At this point the narrator has nothing more to learn about the duke and duchess, and a new theme, homosexuality, enters the narrative.

The juncture of *Le Côté de Guermantes* and *Sodome et Gomorrhe* illustrates rather well Proust's intricate structures, his fondness for interweaving themes. The society theme, by being joined to it in one continuous time unit, is made to turn into the homosexual one, but within the temporal continuum there is a reversal of chronology (the last pages of *Guermantes* and *Sodome* I) for plot purposes and for a further element of design I will examine later. Also, since homosexuality is a more private than public subject, some device must be found to link secret mores and social appearances, as Proust does with the appearances of the baron, first in the afternoon and then in the evening. And perhaps the most surprising device of all is the closure of the society section with "Les Intermittences du coeur," a short reflective interlude dealing with the narrator's memory of his grandmother and with an apple tree in springtime flower, which reminds us of Combray and its values. Proust is emphasizing the confrontation of the themes of innocence and experience. The impact of the thought of his grandmother on the narrator is such that social life will appear to him as "degrading" (2:768).

The thematics of experience have, as their concomitant, the absence of imaginative life and the failure of the narrator's original quest. By now the narrator is no longer even looking for analogues of art in Saint-Loup or for Mme de Guermantes's individuality as a hostess, and from the search for myth and beauty he turns to an especially ugly kind of compulsive behavior as it begins to seem possible that Albertine is indeed a lesbian. The mystery of the Other, alluring, vast, and imprecise in *À l'ombre des jeunes filles en fleurs*, narrows now to a specifically sexual secret, which is not a mystery in the earlier sense at all. The narrator becomes in turn a rather unpleasant inquisitor on various occasions, chilly, obsessed, and indifferent really to Albertine. The automobile demythologizes the countryside at the same time by making every spot quickly accessible; the narrator ceases to think of work and spends his days with Albertine, for whom he feels nothing when calm, and anger when uneasy about her past and activities. The endless cycle of *calme* and *angoisse/anxiété* emprisons him; his subjugation to a kind of sterile emotional determinism dependent on childhood feelings becomes obvious. One day an airplane reminds the narrator of freedom.

In the great brief final chapter of *Sodome*, the narrator alludes to the nature of the Edenic tree when he speaks of "the fatal consequences which evil actions indefinitely engender, not only for those who have committed them, but for those who have done no more, have thought that they were doing no more than look on at a curious and entertaining spectacle, like myself, alas, on that afternoon long ago at Montjouvain, concealed behind a bush where (as when I complacently listened to an account of Swann's love affairs), I had perilously allowed to expand within myself the fatal road, destined to cause me suffering, of Knowledge" (2:1115). The knowledge of good and evil is complemented by the idea of the fall implicit in the *drame du coucher*, which is not mentioned for another page or two, but inevitably comes into this nexus. In "Combray" the episode of Montjouvain is not connected to anything; here we see how it is related to the *drame du coucher*, to which the liaison of Swann and Odette has already been compared.

Some interesting further thematic relations suggest themselves. The narrator had, in the first chapter of *Swann*, stated that the *drame du coucher* was part of his conscious memory. His life as a whole in Combray, on the other hand, was evoked only by the madeleine and linden tea. It is the forgotten quality of the mythic in his life that involuntary memory brought back, a time of innocence and unbounded future freedom. The *drame du coucher*, in contrast, represents determinism and prefigures experience at its worst, the higher imagination being replaced by jealous fantasies. There are two thematic series, both adumbrated in the first chapter of *Swann*: that of vital imaginative perceptions and freedom; and that of bondage to the sterile cycle of jealousy and indifference. It is in the course of *Guermantes* and *Sodome* that a shift occurs, as the quest for the secret of truth and beauty fades out and a progressive knowledge of evil—the germs of which are in the *drame du coucher* and Montjouvain episode—comes to dominate the narrative.

The *drame du coucher* which the narrator relives with Albertine is an archetype, a personal myth in that rather special sense. It is not unfitting that other archetypes supply the opening and closing of *Sodome*: the cities of the plain in Part I and, in II-4, the comparison with Orestes' vengeance, which we have already seen, followed by imagery of a mystic mass.

> I had never seen the dawn of so beautiful or painful a morning. And thinking of all the nondescript scenes that were about to be lighted up, scenes which, only yesterday, would have filled me simply with the desire to visit them, I could not repress a sob when, with a gesture of oblation mechanically performed, which appeared to me to symbolise the bloody sacrifice which I should have to make of all joy, every morning, until the end of my life, a solemn renewal, celebrated as each day dawned, of my daily grief and of the blood from my wound, the golden egg of the sun, as though propelled by the breach of equilibrium brought about at the moment of coagulation by a change in density, barbed with tongues of flame as in a painting, came leaping through the curtain behind which no one had felt that it was quivering with impatience, ready to appear on the scene and to spring aloft, the mysterious, ingrained purple of which it flooded with waves of light [2:1128].

His life is sacrificed by his coming marriage to Albertine, a passion which he explains as the demonic inversion of his old quest for beauty (2:1119). This blood sacrifice of self is the final and most extreme form taken by the narrator's guilt, which he feels he has incurred at the time of his grandmother's death and his subsequent knowledge of Sodom, though of course his guilt can be traced back to the death-bringing victory over his mother pursuant to the *drame du coucher*. This passage, in any case, justifies on grounds of symmetry the "intermittencies of the heart" section, devoted early in *Sodome* (II-1) to the grandmother. In itself, the blood sacrifice, along with Orestes' vengeance and the grandly written initial introduction to Sodom and Gomorrah, attempts to elevate to tragic dignity a narrative which, for much of its length, deals with the comic or, especially as regards the narrator's actions, the merely unpleasant.

After the magnificent conclusion of *Sodome*, the story of the narrator's life with Albertine in *La Prison-*

nière inevitably descends to the same level of manic obsessions I have remarked on in the preceding part. At the same time, however, art occupies a prominent place in the narrator's thoughts for the first time since he studied the duchess's Elstirs near the beginning of *Guermantes* II. After he considers, at home, the possibility that art is a mere technique, hearing the Vinteuil septet at the Verdurins' suggests to him an entirely different train of ideas; he formulates another hypothesis, which might even be called a myth of art. Vinteuil's music, with its language of untranslatable "ideas," gives one to believe that art refers to a lost native land, one of childhood, like Combray, and inaccessible to ordinary memory, or even refers to another existence entirely. Indeed, the passage in *La Prisonnière* on the death of Bergotte affirms that life is led as if another world existed, whether believed in or not. Art, in short, reminds the narrator that his enslavement to jealousy, with its obsession with material facts, is not the only kind of life, but of course the question remains, and is not yet answered, whether he is capable of a higher existence. These thoughts are set forth in *La Prisonnière* but are still unconnected with the narrator's actual life, just as in "Combray" the Montjouvain episode provides a thematic contrast without being tied into the dominant subject matter.

When the narrator visits Venice in *La Fugitive*, there is surprisingly little commentary on the experience. We seem implicitly to be led to feel that this fulfillment of the large design (three other parts of *À la recherche* have concluded with the dream of visiting Venice) is a neutral experience for a narrator gradually forgetting the world of jealousy but not yet open to that of creation. In any case, as an attempt to recapture his myth of life resembling art, it is not a success.

Likewise, the experiences of the heart's intermittencies in regard to Albertine and of involuntary memories of the painful are presented without theoretical elaboration. They are an inversion of his normal experiences of memory, just as the inquest into Albertine's life is an inversion of the search for truth and beauty.

The visit to Combray in *Le Temps retrouvé* demonstrates very obviously the effects on the narrator of aging, experience, and disbelief in his old myth. In the same way, the reading of the manuscript Goncourt journal seems authoritatively to contradict the lesson of the septet and to demonstrate that literature springs not from inner life, but from the mechanical "observation" of which the narrator feels himself incapable. In a more subtle way, the long, nighttime episode in Paris in 1916 demythologizes homosexuality, which had so painfully held his imagination in the worst days with Albertine and which had been treated with tragic elevation at the beginning and end of *Sodome*. This section contains some of the few significantly recurring images in Proust. That of the oriental and therefore sodomitic moon hanging over blacked-out Paris resembles the one on the evening of the princess of Guermantes's party, where the narrator had become consciously aware of homosexuality. In war time the streets contain mostly soldiers on leave in exotic uniforms, and the *Arabian Nights* imagery forms a link with the earlier vision of Sodom. But the end of the evening in Jupien's male brothel reduces the mystery surrounding the baron's walk through the streets to an ordinary routine; the baron visits the "hotel" hoping in vain to have his lower imagination stimulated as much as his flesh. At this point, with the lurid scene at Montjouvain and the maniacal speculations on Albertine's erotic activities so far in the past, it becomes apparent that those obsessive imaginings had perhaps as little to do with the reality they were supposed to uncover as the false *apaches* or tough young men inexpertly playing roles to excite Charlus. Both the lesson of the Vinteuil septet and the jealous visions of Albertine, the domains of the higher and lower forms of imagination, seem to have been false or exaggerated.

"In order to possess what you do not possess you must go by the way of dispossession." A series of paradoxes occur to the narrator as he sits in the princess of Guermantes's library in *Le Temps retrouvé* and meditates on how the quality of his past life can be recaptured. Like the notions of fall and will, these have a para-Christian quality, for the paradox is a characteristic form of evangelical and Pauline wisdom: a past act can be recaptured only by taking account of things having nothing to do with it (3:870); the occurrence of something in both past and present gives not the feeling of time but that of extratemporality (3:871); contact with the past makes one want to live in the present (3:872); the presence of beauty is only perceived when it is absent (3:872); eternity is experienced only briefly (3:875); most of reality is unreal (3:875); our newest and best ideas seem like old ones recurring (3:878); in attempting to capture esthetic impressions, we neglect the essence of the impression (3:891); true life is not life but literature—art contains the perfect image of life, which can be grasped, whereas actual life cannot be seized on (3:895).

After antinomies, paradoxes: while Proust is ready to grant the tenability of antithetical truths or logically inconsistent points of view, like freedom and determinism, he conceives of the highest value as residing in an image created by language, which expresses the ethical content of life and the individuality constituting art. "The ingenuity of the first novelist lay in his understanding that, as the image was the one essential element in the complicated structure of our emotions, so the simplification of it which consisted in the suppression, pure and simple, of 'real' people would be a decided improvement" (1:85). This "image" can best be taken to designate the totality of the work of art, so that in its synthesis are contained the contrasts of myth and experience, of imagery in the local sense and ratiocination. The paradoxes attempt to express the elusive relations between the condensed image and its model, and we sense that their prototype can be considered the losing of life in order to gain it. Salvation through art not surprisingly partakes of the same mystique as Christian soteriology. Moreover, redemption by creativity is the ultimate myth in this world that has discarded Christianity; incidents of mythic perception and the narrator's attempt to live by his myth of the future are comprised within this larger myth, which is coincident with a work of art, as his earlier mythic vision was not. Of course, not every masterpiece can embody such a peremptorily absolute conception of the nature of art and such an alternative to religion.

As is not infrequent with modern writers, I have had to use the words "myth" and "mythic" in more than one sense in talking of Proust, and it is appropriate to review them here. First we have mythic perception as a way of seeing and thinking about experience other than that normally dictated by the Kantian categories that organize an adult's impressions. Causality, the distinctions and relations between persons, words, and things, the attribution of special meaningfulness to the inanimate—all these form different patterns in mythic thinking from what we find in rational-empirical categorizing. It was in Proust's lifetime that anthropologists began studies of such phenomena, and in France one of his contemporaries, Lucien Lévy-Bruhl, became known for his characterization of the "primitive mentality" and its way of seeing nature and the supernatural. Of course, something of this "primitive" mentality is always present in childhood and begins to permeate literature from the romantic period on. One thinks of nature in Shelley, Hölderlin, and the later Victor Hugo, for example. By the time of the French Symbolists, distinctions between metaphor as a mere rhetorical device and as an expression of thought have become harder and harder to make.

As I have noted, Proust's general term for mythic qualities is *mystère*, which might be defined as the disparity between the long tradition of rationalizing accounts of man's duties and goals and experiences which abstract and ethically oriented philosophy, such as that of the seventeenth and eighteenth centuries, is incapable of explaining. Proust's youthful narrator does not hesitate between a view of reality as abstractions embodied in a logical framework and one of reality as various particulars about which one cannot reason, such as the "Persian" church on the sea brink in Balbec, that cannot merely be classified as one example of a certain type of architecture. After keenly scrutinizing the mystery represented by names, people, and landscapes, the narrator concludes that the goal of mythic experience would be to live in a work of art, the one he expects to find in Balbec or elsewhere. There is nothing naive about his realization that art— and this term designates merely a story in words or an image, by no means great art—is the prototype which encourages his inclination to imagine the garden of

Guermantes as totally unlike any garden he has been in. His myths, however, can only come into being amid the favorable circumstances of an advanced society which has lived through a phase of rationalism like the Enlightenment and found it lacking as a total explanation of experience. In that sense, the analogy with primitive mythopoeia, though suggestive, can be misleading.

In modern literature, myth making is not at all the same thing as using myths, although the two on occasion are superimposed. In myths of gods or heroes, the supersession of the rational Kantian categories may be only intermittent, compared with the narrator's vision of the duchess of Guermantes in *À la recherche*, where it is the irrational perceptions that focus our attention. Proust's myths of origins and archetypes—most prominently those of the cities of the plain, Orestes, and the Mass, which frame *Sodome*—are mysterious and inaccessible to logic in a perhaps deeper and certainly different way from the imagery of the duchess perpetually surrounded by her garden and the woods of Guermantes. Furthermore, the most durable classical-heroic and Hebrew myths are highly ethicized, so that in still another way, myth and myth making are both related and yet contrasting. We do not always find that myth and myth making go together in modern literature. James Joyce, for example, uses only the framework of heroic myth in *Ulysses*. Such distinctions can be pursued in the analysis of a good many modern works. The one general characteristic of the use of myths and mythopoeia since the late nineteenth century is the combination of these rather poetic materials with the conventions of realism to produce a texture in which the two elements heighten each other's effect. This may take the form of

violent juxtapositions, as in the works of Ezra Pound
or T. S. Eliot, or else of a more subtle contrast, as in
Proust's themes of myth and experience.

Myths about art, the transfer of reverence from
the traditionally sacred to the esthetic, were an important aspect of French sensibility and thinking on art
in Proust's youth, and we see a late form of the religion
of art in his work; in this, as in some other ways, he
represents a culmination of Symbolist esthetics. In its
more general form, widespread in minor writers, the
idea of art as an object of worship has a very confused
metaphysical status but an unmistakable tone and
imagery: the *sacrum* which is beauty is best represented by a rather bloodless, otherworldly virgin, or
else by a seemingly perverse feminine idol with hints
of the romantic agony. Its moral content is the refusal
of the life-giving. In a more thoughtful way, Mallarmé
conceived of the religion of art as a communion of the
faithful in the worship of the book as absolute, the
synthesis of the being and nothingness whose disarray
composes the universe. Proust disengages himself
from such rarefied notions by placing primary emphasis on the ethical: art is salvation for the individual.
A transcendent basis for morals lies in the as-if world;
we live as if another life and world existed, so that a
moral theology is possible and even necessary, despite
its hypothetical grounding. Such a conception permits
a nonsolipsistic, generally valid moral law and justifies
all soteriological aspirations. The worship of beauty as
an object, especially in the form of one particular set of
images, essentially is eliminated, as is that of any specific book. It is the experience of art, the true life, and the
vision through others' subjectivity that are at the center
of Proust's cult of music, painting, and literature.

2

the techniques of fiction

Point of View and the Individual

Proust has often been praised for his art of creating characters in the nineteenth-century fashion; it has been suggested even that he is the last great master of the art. While this is true in a sense, the creation of fictional people in his novel is much more innovative, complex, and varied in both theory and practice than it may at first seem. One small example of the peculiarities to be met with in Proust's depiction of people: the narrator's family is stylized, so that while his father and grandfather are related (the grandmother entered the father and grandfather's family [1:12]), the narrator's grandmother is the mother's mother. The fourfold grandparents of reality have been reduced to an economical two, and as one follows the references to them in the novel (e.g., 1:75), they shift between the father's and mother's families for the needs of narration, all this being accomplished with great subtlety and elegance of technique, so that few readers have been aware of the discrepancy—which is, of course, what Proust wanted.

The handling of the grandparents is one of those anomalies to be found in the text to which the reader's attention is not drawn, in this novel where so much is commented on. Another such element is the feminization of the narrator. Proust makes much over distinctions between the sexes, so that the mingling or reversal of such characteristics will stand out, as in the case of M. and Mme de Vaugoubert (2:642–46). This notion of attraction through sexual reversal may seem to border on the mythic, but it is sufficiently widespread in late nineteenth-century literature (in *À rebours*, chapter 9, for example, or Zola's *La Curée*) that the reader may be assumed to recognize it in the depiction of the narrator and Albertine in *À l'ombre des jeunes filles en fleurs*. The narrator is presented as rather feminine in relation to Saint-Loup (1:869; cf. 1:780), Albertine as boyish. This does not mean anything in regard to the genesis of the novel, but simply emphasizes one more curious aspect of the way characters are presented with only partial commentary.

The narrator's decision to comment on something he has not been aware of is not always a simple matter of saying, in Balzacian style, "Here is why . . . " at the beginning of a paragraph and taking advantage of his privileged position. One of the most characteristic devices is for the narrator merely to slip in, often by means of an accessory pluperfect tense, some information that he presents neither as purposefully withheld up to that point or of such moment that it deserves narration for its own sake. For example: "Robert de Saint-Loup, whom his mother had succeeded in separating from his mistress after painful, abortive attempts . . . had written me a letter in which he announced his arrival in France" (2:348). What this creates is a change in perspective for the reader and a feeling that the narrator's experience is more varied and complex than the novel allows. The greatest of all such casual introductions of unsuspected events comes near the end. "The Princess of Guermantes had, in fact, died and it was the former Mme Verdurin that the prince . . . had married" (3:955). An equal feeling of density of incident comes from the occasional glimpses into a future which is never again mentioned, as when the narrator remarks on "the Princess of Guermantes, with whom I did not know I was to have such close relations one day" (2:714). Or again: "For the moment let us leave aside the men who have concluded a pact with Gomorrah. We shall speak of them when M. de Charlus comes to know them" (2:623).

The narrator's casual omniscience, his knowledge, for example, of a very private conversation between two people or, occasionally, of what someone says to himself, has disturbed critics, for a strict interpretation of point of view has bedeviled much commentary on fiction. The major modern novelists who are often assumed to be concerned with strict point of view are not always so single-minded. Joyce's *Ulysses* contains seemingly fortuitous shifts from one character to another and examples of unexpected omniscience; *What Maisie Knew*, so regularly cited as one of Henry James's most thoroughgoing experiments in point of view, shows, as James admitted, authorial commentary independent of Maisie's thoughts and far better informed than she is. The problem with excessive concern over point of view is that one loses sight of the fact that it is an abstract criterion divorced from style, and that verbal texture is ultimately the more valid basis for analyzing fiction. Proust saw the problem quite clearly and insisted on the prime importance of unity of style, the principle he learned from Flaubert and which is also at the center of Joyce's and James's actual practice as writers. The superstition of point of view could even be termed a naively realistic misconception. In any case, Proust's handling of point of view can be said to be neither primarily limited nor omniscient: the effect of his novel depends on a judicious, subtle mingling of both techniques. The enigma of characters we can never totally understand must be balanced by our being able to pierce their mystery at times, so that subjectivity does not turn into solipsism and so that we have some idea of what kind of facts might lie behind the mystery. It is the contrastive effect that is widespread in Proust's working out of his novel; opposing techniques are used to heighten one another, and all is in their method of combination.

Sometimes the most interesting questions of truth and falsehood are not the object of any remark, while elsewhere the narrator indicates that this or that statement or putative event is of unascertainable truth or reality. The narrator does not comment when Albertine claims hardly to know Mlle Vinteuil and her friend, thus rendering pointless much of the action of *La Prisonnière* (3:337). Likewise, Charlus, for no perceptible reason, tells a story of Swann and Odette's meeting that is completely at variance with what the narrator has told us (3:299–301). Elsewhere, the narrator suggests that things have multiple causes and multiple ends, thus obviating the most ordinary kinds of explanations (1:939; 3:615).

Quite apart from the usual questions of fictional technique—how does the narrator know what the

Verdurins said to each other in secret about Saniette, or why was the duke of Châtellerault nervous on seeing the valet he had met in the Champs-Élysées?— there are theoretical considerations on the nature of personality which play an important role in Proust's depiction of characters. The discontinuity of personality is a favorite theme, and the narrator's uncertain grasping for his own identity in the opening pages of *Swann* is a prelude to the difficulty he will experience in defining just what traits certain characters have at any given moment. While there is some prerational, animal sense of life in the depths of the mind (1:5), at a more conscious level there is a succession of *I*'s; personality is a series of mental events. The actual use of this idea in novelistic terms is varied. The narrator's family members hardly show any change of direction, but Albertine is so unstable as barely to form a "character" in the traditional manner of fiction. In *La Prisonnière* and especially in *La Fugitive*, there is much insistence on discontinuity of personality in the narrator and in Albertine as they experience crises (3:91, 92, 104, 119, 426, 430, 432, 529, 594). Proust even explains in what way Albertine is not a conventional novelistic character (1:894–95). There are characters on the other hand, like Legrandin, who follow the pattern of traditional comedy in consistently manifesting some mechanical principle of behavior; portraiture of the older sort, with reflections of a moral-psychological nature, is brilliantly illustrated by Mlle Vinteuil, who never becomes a real character in the novel. There is great subtlety in what is left unsaid in depicting the duchess of Guermantes: the most important fact about her personality is that she has never had a lover or children and the duke does not care for her in any personal way. One of her most revealing actions, her systematic persecution of the footman who is happily engaged (2:493), receives no comment.

At the same time as he maintains that personality is a series of mental events, Proust refers to psychological laws, which would seem to infringe on the individuality of the shifting *I*. Here, of course, Proust's antinomial distinction is relevant between higher and lower truths, between the images which are the content of the mind and the laws or maxims which may be predicated about it. By these psychological laws the action of *La Prisonnière* is foretold (1:563), and that of *La Fugitive* as well (1:305; 3:87).

While the simultaneous taste for concrete detail and abstract formulation is a principle of Proust's thought and one whose coherence he defended expressly, the more striking stylistic effects occur in efforts to render individuality. The speech, opinions, gestures, clothes, and general exterior of the character is the object of enormous care on Proust's part, surpassing that of any previous French novelist, and for good theoretical reasons. The necessity of showing the character in an actual moment which catches the shifting manifestations of personality relates Proust's work, furthermore, to the rule, much admired in the English-speaking world, of portraying emotions rather than telling of them. Proust had formulated the theory of representational as opposed to summary technique in regard to Balzac's fiction and to phrases like "he had a sublime expression"; the full application of it, however, was to lead in his novel to an extraordinary series of stylistic performances, not quite like anything we usually associate with "showing not telling."

The eye is the most important feature in Proust's descriptions of faces. Remembering that another person is noumenal, a thing-in-itself, we see that the eye is a kind of window through which we may catch a glimpse of what is hidden in the person's mind.

> But, at the sound of the word Guermantes, I saw in the middle of each of our friend's [Legrandin's] blue eyes a little brown dimple appear, as though they had been stabbed by some invisible pin-point, while the rest of his pupils, reacting from the shock, received and secreted the azure overflow. His fringed eyelids darkened, and drooped. His mouth, which had been stiffened and seared with bitter lines, was the first to recover, and smiled, while his eyes still seemed full of pain, like the eyes of a handsome martyr whose body bristles with arrows.
> "No, I do not know them," he said [1:127].

These are superperceptions, going well beyond what one can actually see in another person's eyes. Proust effaces the line between description and metaphor when he presents characters; they often, for example, undergo metamorphosis or reflect their heredity. The second sentence following is typical of Proust; another writer might have used an "as if." "Mme de Guermantes had sat down. Her name, accompanied as it was by her title, added to her corporeal dimensions the duchy which projected itself round about her and brought the shadowy, sun-splashed coolness of the woods of Guermantes into this drawing room, to surround the ottoman on which she was sitting" (2:204).

All this imagery is not merely the work of a "flute player," as Norpois calls Bergotte. Toward the end of the novel the narrator reflects on the validity of the notion of an individual personality. To begin with, discontinuity of personality implies that the idea of the individual as a compact unit is questionable. Then, the individual himself may feel divided: in "Un Amour de Swann," the narrator and Swann himself feel that jealousy is an entity which has been added to him and from which he can distinguish himself. Of course, the poetic tradition since Petrarch has talked of "his jealousy overcoming him" and such, but the consistency of this kind of expression in "Un Amour de Swann" and elsewhere suggests more than a mere way of speaking. There are consequently subindividual units, which any analysis of the mind cannot ignore.

There are also other relevant distinctions. For example, a person's social existence may be so strong as to suppress all individuality, in which case the unit is a group or class, like the band of girls in Balbec (3:970). Proust also suggests that events like the Cambremer and Saint-Loup marriages are more significant than the parties concerned (3:972). Finally, superindividual units like the family genetic chain or the "race" (in Proust's rather varied senses) may be vastly more important than any particular ego in the pattern (3:943). When we take into consideration these ideas on the dimensions and limits of the individual, the proliferation of superperceptions, and the appearance in a person of psychological traits we hardly think of as having physical correspondences, we find the justification for much in Proust's style which we might otherwise assume to have no further aim than elegance or wit. This is one of several aspects of his novel that are commented on in the work itself. Bergotte remarks, "You see, he [Norpois] has to keep his mouth shut half the time so as not to use up all the stock of inanities that holds his shirt-front down and his white waistcoat up" (1:562), and "He [Cottard] will find that you have a dilated stomach; he has no need to examine you for it, since he has it already in his eye. You can see it there, reflected in his glasses" (1:570). The narrator is wearied by this complicated language. "This manner of speaking tired me greatly; I said to myself, with the stupidity of common sense: 'There is no more any dilated stomach reflected in Professor Cottard's glasses than there are inanities stored behind the white waistcoat of M. de Norpois' " (1:571).

The stupidity of common sense, however, does not prevail with the narrator, and he tends to see characters in an even more complicated way than Bergotte. "When she [Vinteuil's daughter] had spoken, she would at once take her own words in the sense in which her audience must have heard them, she would be alarmed at the possibility of a misunderstanding, and one would see, in clear outline, as though in a transparency, beneath the mannish face of the 'good sort' that she was, the finer features of a young woman in tears" (1:113). The double person is an especially striking example of the fact that the individual is not altogether the unit we are accustomed to think of him as being.

> When it is a Charlus, whether he is noble or plebeian, that is stirred by such a sentiment of instinctive and atavistic politeness to strangers, it is always the spirit of a relative of the female sex, attendant like a goddess, or incarnate as a double, that undertakes to introduce him into a strange drawing-room and to mould his attitude until he comes face to face with his hostess . . . . As for M. de Charlus, whom the society in which he had lived furnished, at this critical moment, with different examples, with other patterns of affability, and above all with the maxim that one must, in certain cases, when dealing with people of humble rank, bring into play and make use of one's rarest graces, which one normally holds in reserve, it was with a flutter, archly, and with the same sweep with which a skirt would have enlarged and impeded his waddling motion that he advanced upon Mme Verdurin with so flattered and honored an air that one would have said that to be taken to her house was for him a supreme favor. One would have thought that it was Mme de Marsantes who was entering the room [2:907–8].

In the following example, the second person in the double individual is one from a past time of life.

> He [Saint-Loup] did not know them, or their names even, and seeing that they appeared to be extremely intimate with his mistress he could not help wondering whether she too might not once have had, had not still perhaps her place in a life of which he had never dreamed, utterly different from the life she led with him, a life in which one had women for a louis apiece, whereas he was giving more than a hundred thousand francs a year to Rachel. He caught only a fleeting glimpse of that life, but saw also in the thick of it a Rachel other than her whom he knew, a Rachel like the two little tarts in the train, a twenty-franc Rachel. In short, Rachel had for the moment duplicated herself in his eyes, he had seen, at some distance from his own Rachel, the little tart Rachel, the real Rachel, assuming that Rachel the tart was more real than the other [2:162].

"Metaphor" or "simile" is too weak a term to characterize such style; it is apparent that Proust is far more daring in his practice of figurative language than his brief, if important, remarks in praise of metaphor would suggest. He is moving in the direction of the kind of phenomenological description Sartre attempts somewhat later in *La Nausée* and which is the philosophically justified form of the irreducible individuality of vision upon which Proust makes art rest.

The problem of fictional characters I have been examining presented itself at first in terms of the most traditional question of technique: the means by which we know the contents of the minds of the narrator and his characters. This is a basically mimetic kind of question and most appropriate to the nineteenth-century novel. More recent fiction, like Nathalie Sarraute's, has destroyed the discreteness and wholeness of the character and needs to be approached differently. With Proust, however, we find a range of effects.

There is a basic core of character portrayals which are brilliant and traditional. At the same time, Proust tends, if not to destroy his characters, yet certainly to modify them, sometimes radically, and to invest them with peculiar qualities of uncertainty. The closer we look at what happens to the conception or presentation of characters in Proust, the more we are drawn into stylistic observations. We have to notice the surprising pluperfects giving us a new perspective on the past, or the use of imagistic language which cannot be reduced to an illustrative comparison. We become aware that something like the attitudes and expectations we bring to the modernist poetry of the earlier twentieth century will often constitute the most appropriate way to read Proust's language. But before I attempt an analysis primarily of verbal techniques, there remains one other traditional category of fictional technique to be considered, that concerned with plot—or, in any event, with actions arranged in a temporal pattern.

Time, Tension, and Causality

Proust speaks in *La Prisonnière* of those great nineteenth-century artists like Honoré de Balzac and Richard Wagner, who discovered the shape and unity of their masterworks only after they were well into the writing of them. Like so many other remarks in *À la recherche*, his comment applies to his own work, whose length and shape were totally changed after the publication of *Swann*. As a result, the character of *Swann* was retrospectively modified. Parts acquire some of their significance only from the structure of the whole, and this is particularly true of the temporal pattern, which is now a lengthy introduction to a much longer work. The movement of *Swann* is justified for us now because it is only the first of seven parts, and by no means an overly long one for an introduction.

Traditionally fiction had used an arbitrary, created time frame, involving a moment of beginning and a moment of ending, so that a piece of fictive reality, however great the sense of temporal realism, was lifted out of the larger, indefinite sweep of time. First-person narrative was no exception. The *passé composé* tense of the first line of *À la recherche* ("Longtemps, je me suis couché de bonne heure") sounds as if it might lead to the establishment of the traditional double time reference of first-person stories: a time when the *I* is narrating—a present—and the past of the story. Such a double reference is implied in the *passé composé* as in no other past tense. But as we read, the present, or at least the more recent period of time, becomes elusive. Allusions to it recur at the end of "Combray," in the last pages of *Swann*, and occasionally later, but only in *Le Temps retrouvé* do we realize that we can never place it. And by that time we realize as well that the novel's ending refers back to itself, so that we could never describe it as a horizontal line of temporal development intersected by the two lines of beginning and end.

The difficulty of ascertaining even relative time in "Combray" is complicated by indications such as a mere "once" or "one year" for a specific anecdote, while the predominant tense is the imperfect, which of course cannot mark inception or terminal action. Gérard Genette sees Proust's major innovation in temporal patterns as the substitution of the alternation *imperfect/preterite scene* for the *summary narration/preterite scene* duality normal in most novelists. (See *Figures III* [Paris: Seuil, 1972].) Much of the imperfect usage falls into an aspectual category peculiar to Proust: the imperfect is not so much iterative as what may best be called "typical." In this typical imperfect, conversations may be as specific as Aunt Léonie and Françoise's exchanges about an unfamiliar dog in the street or some asparagus, but the basic verbs, those of speaking, are *disait*, *répondait*, and so forth.

> "Françoise, if you had come in five minutes ago, you would have seen Mme Imbert go past with some asparagus twice the size of what old mother Callot has: do try to find out from her cook where she got them. . . ."
> "I shouldn't be surprised if they came from the Curé's," Françoise would say, and:
> "I'm sure you wouldn't, my poor Françoise," my aunt would reply shrugging her shoulders. "From the Curé's indeed! You know perfectly well that he can never grow anything but wretched little twigs of asparagus" [1:55].

Proust did not conceive of his typical imperfect as totally stagnant in temporal reference; although a sequence of days can hardly be narrated in it because of the natural inertia of the imperfect, the progression of the season can be superimposed on it. The outline of the seasonal movement is hazy enough to be accommodated to the tense. Thus in "Combray" the various elements of narrative are first organized into a long Sunday, stretching from cool weather in the morning and Holy Week, to warm days in the afternoon around the time of Ascension or Rogation days. After the account of this major cycle of life and occupations in Combray comes that of a minor cycle—Saturday, with its special routine—and then, through a description of the hawthorn flowers in church during May, we move back to Sunday. The hawthorns (and fruit tree blossoms) are a recurrent seasonal point of reference in Proust's novel and are given great prominence here.

Descriptions of them continue into the early part of the walk on the Méséglise (Swann's) way; Proust sometimes likes to avoid sharp breaks in narrative texture by employing some theme or image that will overlap the two units.

The substantial section devoted to the Méséglise way is constructed of the small building blocks Proust tends to use and whose pattern is often overlooked. The Méséglise way has as landmarks Tansonville, Swann's estate, which the narrator's family avoids passing too near; the plain; Montjouvain, Vinteuil's house; the Roussainville woods; and the church of Saint-André-des-Champs, where strollers can take refuge in the event—a very frequent one—of rain. The one time the narrator's family walks along the edge of Tansonville, something happens which gives rise to various scenes, all of which are recounted as part of the walk; these constitute what might be called a digression except that it is part of the main substance of the story. When the passage about the Méséglise way is examined closely, it turns out to be divided into two subcycles referring to different general areas of time and taking account of the weather. Then, if we attempt to find some further order in the small units Proust is building with, it becomes apparent that the movement is not in the least associative or "musical" or whatever, but consists rather in enumerations with alternatives. It can be represented in the following way:

Méséglise: The Short Walk

I. Early years; summer; narrator walks with family; walk taken even in threatening weather
    A. Tansonville
        1. Tansonville is avoided
        2. One day they pass by Tansonville; scenes

    B. Landscape
    C. Montjouvain
       1. Vinteuil and his daughter
       2. Vinteuil, his daughter, and her friend after a certain year
    D. After Montjouvain
       1. Good weather; walk on plain
       2. Rain
          a. Refuge in woods
          b. Refuge in portal of Saint-André-des-Champs
    E. Return home

  II. Later years; autumn; narrator walks alone and goes out even when it is actually raining
    A. Tansonville, plain, and Montjouvain
    B. Woods; cries, "Zut, zut, zut," at sight of beauty; erotic dreams, unfulfilled
    C. Return home

III. Much later period; Montjouvain

The largest organizing principle here is that of succession in time, and we feel the passage of years as the second subcycle of walks begins.

> If the weather was bad all morning, my family would abandon the idea of a walk, and I would remain at home. But, later on, I formed the habit of going out by myself on such days, and walking toward Méséglise-la Vineuse, during the autumn when we had to come to Combray to settle the division of my Aunt Léonie's estate; for she had died at last [1:153].

Now the narrator's concerns are more erotic. In one further episode of the Méséglise way, "several years" after the second cycle of walks, Vinteuil is dead. (This is the *artiste du mal* scene of the daughter and her friend profaning his photograph; 1:159–65.)

In the account of the Guermantes way, which has an associative pattern, the description of the walk along the river leads to reflections on the mythic character of its headwaters and on the almost as mythic character of the castle of Guermantes and its duke and duchess. The narrator regrets his lack of talent as a writer, which might lead him to know the duchess; he writes a prose poem on the steeples of Martinville without really connecting that effort of translating an impression with his preconceived ideas of literature. Here in the episode of the Guermantes way we find truly associative movement in the themes, and it is quite appropriate, the burden of the passage being the narrator's illusions or delusions about life and literature; it is the movement of dreams. There is no significant use of time, and the eroticism is sublimated in this world of revery and false conceptions. The narrator's prose poem marks some advance over merely crying "Zut, zut, zut," in the presence of beauty, but we should not take the arrangement of the two ways as necessarily representing a progression.

The narrator gives to the two ways "the cohesion, the unity which belongs only to creations of our mind" (1:134), and it is significant that he employs different structural patterns for each. The mass of material pertaining to the Méséglise way is highly organized according to the logical principles of succession in place and time. The profusion of detail, as in the scenes connected with Tansonville, does not, however hypertrophic, destroy this arrangement. The lack of forward movement in the Guermantes way, on the other hand, makes it the more suitable section with which to close "Combray." Both episodes illustrate Proust's use of multiple subdivision, the accretive kind of structure that looks as if it could be truncated at any point. A large range of relations, however, can determine the exact order of the blocks. Even lack of relation can be significant, as in the absence of real connection between the *artiste du mal* episode and what precedes it. Temporally and thematically it is separate, and its genuine importance will not be understood for many hundreds of pages. This, of course, brings to mind some of the more elaborate poetic structures of the late nineteenth and the twentieth centuries, for Proust is essentially using the same general notions of structure as are found in Rainer Maria Rilke's *Duineser Elegien* or Paul Valéry's *La Jeune Parque*: small units are preferred in order to obtain continual effects of contrast, profusion, change of direction, temporary enigma, or concentration, instead of a sustained texture. The logical fullness of the Méséglise way section is perceived subliminally well before one establishes it through analysis, and similarly the tangential, dreamlike movement of the Guermantes way is received first as an impression. When we have understood how Proust's multiple subdivisions work in "Combray," encompassing a full range from elements of conventional order to the alogical, we are better prepared to follow the elaborate temporal patterns of many later parts of *À la recherche*.

Proust manifestly did not wish us to substitute an exact model of real time for his fictional time. (A sophisticated and detailed discussion of the question of real time and Proust's novel can be found in Gareth H. Steel, *Chronology and Time in "À la recherche du temps perdu"* [Geneva: Drox, 1979].) Thus key events which are referred to but not represented in the novel may be impossible to situate so many years from this or that event described. For example, since the marriage of Swann and Odette takes place when the narrator is a child and knows nothing of it, it must be situated somewhere between the period of time he remembers and real historical time. The whole episode of "Un Amour de Swann" is characteristic of Proust's temporal inventiveness. At the beginning of "Un Amour," the initial stages of Odette and Swann's liaison are played out against the background of snow (1:219), winter (1:221), and a cold spring (1:235). At the end of spring (1:274) occurs Swann's break with the Verdurins. We have, therefore, the first half of a not very detailed time frame; Proust's ingeniousness will be to leave the end of the story temporally open, so that "years of my [Swann's] life" will pass (with episodes, to be sure) in a kind of grey, indistinct atmosphere and with no hint of the ending which the action is to have in Swann and Odette's marriage.

There is an obvious risk of monotony in the method of "Un Amour de Swann." Proust avoids it with a brilliant invention that represents his imagination at its best. Well over halfway through "Un Amour" Swann goes to a *soirée musicale*, which opens with extraordinary descriptions like nothing else in the chapter. Here is a footman: "A few feet away, a great strapping lad in livery stood musing, motionless, statuesque, useless, like that purely decorative warrior whom one sees in the most tumultuous of Mantegna's paintings, lost in dreams, leaning upon his shield, while all around him are fighting and bloodshed and death; detached from the group of his companions who were thronging about Swann, he seemed as determined to remain unconcerned with the scene, which he followed vaguely with his cruel, greenish eyes, as if it had been the Massacre of the Innocents or the Martyrdom of Saint James" (1:323–24). Swann meets people from his milieu whom he has not seen for a long time, preoccupied as he has been by Odette; the change in style and the representation of sophisticated speech serve, more than any mere notation of time could, to put into the distance Swann's involvement with the Verdurins and Odette. Vivid, concrete imagery makes us feel the diverting reality of Swann's life in aristocratic society and the lengthy emptiness which the chapter has recorded up to this point. It seems a fitting conclusion to the *soirée* that Swann realizes the hopelessness of his relations with Odette. Structurally, the *soirée* is the first example of a pattern characteristic of Proust's narrative technique: into an extended episode or chapter he inserts a contrasting section, so that the form of the whole can be represented as *A B A*. This device always creates impressive effects, sharpening our perceptions of the opposing themes, scenes, or situations.

The ending of *Swann* is a last-minute addition to the work, which had to be cut at an awkward point, the last chapter of *Swann* and the first of *À l'ombre des jeunes filles en fleurs* being continuous. Proust showed a great writer's ability to make a material hindrance the starting point for a new esthetic conception and order. The new conclusion of *Swann*, which forms an *A B A* arrangement with what precedes and what follows, is a false cadence in contrast to the madeleine episode.

> The reality that I had known no longer existed. It sufficed that Mme Swann did not appear, in the same attire and at the same moment, for the whole avenue to be altered. The places that we have known belong now only to the little world of space on which we map them for our own convenience. None of them was ever more than a thin slice, held between the contiguous impressions that composed our life at that time; remembrance of a particular form is but regret for a particular moment; and houses, roads, avenues are as fugitive, alas, as the years" [1:427].

The elegiac regrets over passing fashions and fleeting years are a product of the uncreative, voluntary memory, as opposed to the earlier, happy conjuring up of all of Combray. "Philosophical *vanitas*," as Proust called the lament over time's passage, is not the way of a true *recherche du temps perdu*.

In the account of Norpois's coming to dinner in "Autour de Mme Swann," we have a well-developed *passé simple* episode, the center of an arrangement contrasting with the slow passages dealing with minor events, such as the narrator's playing with Gilberte in the Champs-Élysées and dreams about her. The Norpois dinner is not only the second long social occasion in *À la recherche*, it is the first example of interweaving narration, the visit to the theater being told as part of it. In the framing Champs-Élysées episodes, the narrator's efforts toward furthering his quest of truth and beauty through Gilberte, which consist of writing letters to her and to her father, have no result. The quality of stagnant time is broken only by Cottard's unintentional intervention, which brings about an invitation from Gilberte. Shortly thereafter, at a luncheon where he meets Bergotte, his quest is at an end, since Bergotte always lay behind his love for Gilberte. As is evident from this summary, passivity and a penchant for dreaming dominate him, and hazy temporality renders his mental state. From "Noms de pays: Le Nom" through "Autour de Mme Swann," two summers are suppressed in the narrative, and New Year's Day, which should give the feeling of time renewed but no longer does for the narrator, is the one temporal point that stands out. The elimination of summer—not a word in the narrative betrays its necessarily having intervened—is an excellent example of Proust's manipulation of fictional time to adjust it to some thematic design. The real action of the chapters, that for which the narrator is responsible and not a series of coincidences and purely fortuitous causes, can be very briefly stated. After becoming a close friend, Gilberte grows tired of the narrator, for reasons explained much later (3:134); he then resolves, in one short line, never to see her again. Once, weakening, he sets off to call on her, but he is turned back by the sight of her with a young man. In other words, the separation can be described as an act of will on the narrator's part, followed by one "nervous impulse," which has, however, no consequences. Aside from all the meditations on relationships and sketches of the role of fashion in Odette's world, the story of À *l'ombre* is an illustration of the narrator's will, weakened since the night in Combray when his mother gave in to his "nervous" demands, but not yet hopelessly vitiated, as it will be later on. He is not yet totally the victim of psychological determinism.

As we have had the occasion to observe, there is a limited element of intentionality in the action of "Autour de Mme Swann"; that is to say, the portion of it in which the narrator perceives some goal in his life—penetrating Gilberte's mysterious and beautiful existence—is but the first half of the entire narrative. Moreover, the intentionality manifest in the narrator's behavior is largely ineffectual, and chance plays an important role. Generally, our idea of plot depends on the intentional factor, working often in an elaborate counterpoint with coincidence and good or bad luck. Since the time of Flaubert and his disciples, authors have experimented with fictive characters deliberately lacking in aims, but usually the resulting antiplot is intended to suggest some large and commonly pessimistic truth about life. Proust's novel, however, is not in the least pessimistic after the manner of the naturalists. The half of "Autour de Mme Swann" taking place after the abrupt, briefly told break with Gilberte contains melancholy observations, but it also betrays a great enjoyment of material amenities and the progress of fashion. The fact is simply that the main narrative is still not to begin; *À l'ombre* is a second, more detailed introduction to the world of *À la recherche* after the images of Combray and the account of Swann and Odette. The narrator's infatuation with Gilberte is still an adolescent's story, still a preparatory sketch of his temperament and his first contact with conspicuously fashionable people; it is in the restricted intentionality of the action, the abundant passages in the iterative and typical imperfect, that we see Proust deliberately creating a movement that is generally too leisurely for plot. No one would mistake "Combray" for anything but an introduction, but it is equally important to see how in *À l'ombre* Proust is still primarily making his fictional world denser, rather than concatenating events.

The narrator's stay in Balbec in "Noms de pays: Le Pays" can be referred to his earlier dreams of the sea and a Romanesque, almost "Persian" church. Very little is made of this, however, and we find the characteristic combination of nonintentional narrative with relaxed, casual time indications of the "one day," "once" sort. Coincidences dominate the first part of the chapter, where the narrator and his grandmother meet and enjoy the company of Mme de Villeparisis, Saint-Loup, and Charlus. This is the kind of texture which made some critics talk of charming memoirs, impressionistic sketches, or other subnovelistic genres. Of course, if we truncated *À la recherche* and read only the first two or three parts, we would completely miss the effect of relaxed temporality as opposed to later narrative tension.

After the appearance of the band of girls on the beach, the narrator is taken with the desire to know them, and some degree of plot is created, which, however, dissipates in time with meeting them. But Proust gave the center of "Noms de pays: Le Pays" a distinctive structure, which joins the earlier aristocratic subject with that of the girls by interweaving narration. "That day," *ce jour-là*, begins the almost exactly central episode, and we immediately feel the emphasis given by the demonstrative in comparison with the multitudes of "one day" and "once." The narrator sees the *jeunes filles en fleurs*, and the length of the meditation they inspire (some ten printed pages) immediately makes us sense their coming importance. The narrator goes to his room, after asking the elevator boy for the list of newly arrived guests, and stops a moment, before entering, to look through the corridor window. This is one of those passages, like Swann's arrival at the *soirée musicale*, where the detail gives a quality of heightened reality to some simple action, in contrast to the curt, schematic character it would normally have in fiction. Sometimes such passages have the peculiarity of taking as long to read as the action would take to perform. These moments illustrate the uneven, unpredictable character of our awareness, which fastens at times onto what we would ordinarily consider insignificant and yet fails to take in completely the events deemed important by reason or intelligence.

As the narrator gazes out of the windows of his room, time starts shifting.

> Regularly, as the season advanced, the picture that I found there in my window changed. At first it was broad daylight and dark only if the weather was bad. . . .

Presently the days grew shorter and at the moment when I entered my room, the violet sky seemed branded with the stiff, geometrical, traveling, effulgent figure of the sun (like the representation of some miraculous sign, of some mystical apparition). . . . A few weeks later, when I went upstairs, the sun had already set [1:802–3].

Suddenly, "there was a knock," and we are back on the day when the narrator saw the girls on the beach. The narrator goes as planned to dinner at Rivebelle with Saint-Loup, and that long passage moves into the imperfect and dinners late in the season. After returning to the hotel and going to sleep in iterative or typical narrative time, he wakes on a specific day, the one after he had seen the girls on the beach. In a surprising move through the *passé composé* to present reflection, we have a kind of analysis of the girls as a group, stressing its predominance over their individuality. Then Saint-Loup's stay in Balbec is at an end, just as they meet Elstir the painter one evening at Rivebelle, who will introduce the narrator to Albertine and her friends.

Thus, in the center of "Noms de pays: Le Pays," there is a transition from Saint-Loup to Albertine, and a rich composite image, complete with present reflections, of the girls on the beach, the seascape, and the narrator's evenings. Temporal contiguity of the picture of the girls and memories of dinner at Rivebelle is made even denser by the blurred superimposition of various moments of the season. Here the main technical device is not so much the juxtaposition of preterite and imperfect, although that plays a role, but the perturbation of sequential narration. Proust is making a whole out of what rationally is disparate material. There are several advantages to what he has done. First of all, there are a good many beginnings in the chapter (principally meeting people), but no ends (except for Saint-Loup's departure); there are likewise no structured events except going to Rivebelle for dinner. Proust has given a distinct central action to the chapter, and, in the reduced scale of the action, suggests the temporal progress of the season, which otherwise would be a rather diffuse process to relate. And, finally, the shape of the whole chapter acquires an *A B A* pattern with respect to the relaxed temporality which precedes and follows the nucleus.

There is a fine example of Proust's typical narration in the imperfect in the opening of *Le Côté de Guermantes*. Françoise's reactions to life in the new apartment provide essential exposition, but the description of them is far more alive than the summary narration traditionally used to convey such information. The passages involving her have the vividness of scenes while creating the density of discursive writing. A logical exposition would be thin in comparison.

Once it is granted that the narrator now lives in the same building as the Guermantes, there is only one chance event in Part I, his being given the theater ticket for the same evening that the duchess goes to hear Mme Berma. Otherwise, this narrative is distinguished from the preceding parts of *À la recherche* by the long-range intentionality governing it. The narrator pursues the duchess with his dreams and attentions for most of Part I, the temporal spread of which is six or eight months. We have now entered the long central story of *À la recherche*, and the absence of periods of stagnant time and undirected action is quite noticeable. The seasonal progress is also more sharply defined than in *À l'ombre* I; the late autumn weather is described in the Doncières section, the passage of winter noted in a few words (2:140–42) which suffice to

orient us, and spring is indicated by the striking description of an apple tree in bloom.

A strong element of intentionality does not necessarily mean that the plot arrives at the point the main
character is seeking. The narrator's trip to Doncières,
to approach the duchess through her nephew, fails,
and while his attending Mme de Villeparisis's *matinée*
does bring him into contact with Mme de Guermantes,
their relations are not in any sense advanced by it. The
futile outcome of intentionality is a plot device to be
used again in *À la recherche*. The first extensive use of
this element of narrative structure is *L'Éducation senti-
mentale*, and it is curious how different the results are
in Flaubert and in Proust.

Much of *Guermantes* I takes place on a long day
when the narrator has lunch with Saint-Loup and
Rachel, stops by the theater with them, goes to Mme
de Villeparisis's *matinée*, and talks with Charlus on the
street afterward. The long day is a Balzacian device,
and it has an obvious advantage: varied kinds of episodes can be grouped together, giving the reader a
sense of coherence. Proust's long day is thus a natural
unit of time which we perceive as having an at least
elementary structure and tensions, related to the narrator's cycle of energy, so that the episodes are held
together by more than just temporal contiguity. This is
especially important because Proust's long day contains not only incidents but much exposition—often
omniscient—and anecdote mingled with the dialogue
and observations of the narrator. The dialogue usually
has little plot function, being used primarily to characterize. In a sense this day has such varied content and
texture as hardly to be called a series of scenes in the
Balzacian manner, which have a closer affinity to
dramaturgical technique. There is a distinct nonthe-

atrical element in Proust's novel, which makes any comparison with Balzac's scenes and the stage utterly useless and misleading. In a true novelistic scene of the conventional sort, there would be no way of conveying all the information Proust provides, so that "fragments of scenes elaborated by commentary" would perhaps be the better description of Proust's method.

This aspect of Proust's narrative is nicely illustrated by the end of the *matinée*. Walking in the street while the baron looks for a cab and gives a long speech patterned on Vautrin's in *Le Père Goriot*, the narrator relates how Bloch père and Mme Sazerat meet and what cab the baron finally chooses. All this seems disproportionate to the few steps the baron and narrator are taking, and the episode trails off just as had the *matinée* in the salon. The narrator goes home, finds the servants in a heated discussion of the Dreyfus case, and goes up to see his ailing grandmother. The conclusion of the day seems amorphous for a novel, as do the ends of other long days or social events in Proust's work. He comments in a number of places about how worthless and unsatisfying social life is, and about the Guermantes's dislike of saying goodnight or putting an end to these occasions, which always leave one hungry for real intellectual and spiritual nourishment. Proust seems regularly to indicate this aimlessness by the many incidental and seemingly irrelevant conversations occurring as a day drifts to an end, as for example, the discussion about ice cream after Swann has left in "Combray" (1:34), the remarks after Norpois has come to dinner (1:481–83), or the exchange with the narrator's parents after the luncheon where he has met Bergotte (1:573–75). Later there will be the elevator boy in Balbec or other servants and their observations. These fatiguing returns home and sometimes idiotic remarks are thoroughly unscenic, in the sense that the big events are not brought to an elegant finish, like the ends of acts on the stage from which conclusions might be drawn. In general, the scenes in Proust's novel do not conform to the realist tradition of impersonal narration contained in a clearly designed frame or setting, which may be stationary or progressive, with characters confronting each other or with situations in well-shaped units. That conception of the scene gives way to a texture made out of far more varied elements. Dialogue, reported thoughts in their surroundings, and description are the elements of the realist scene, an essentially more visual and theatrical esthetic of the novel, whereas anecdotes, digressions, and a very large number of characters, often speaking fragmentarily, are essential to Proust's technique.

It is characteristic of Proust's compositional practice that we do not realize the thematic importance of the grandmother's final illness and death in *Guermantes* II-1 as we read it. We perceive the account of her stroke as an exceptionally fine example of a rather traditional, dramatic, but understated scene, which is of the kind often called "direct" or "simple" because we do not find any conspicuously modernist techniques in it.

> "There is not the slightest hope," he [the professor of medicine] informed me. "It is a stroke brought on by uraemia. In itself, uraemia is not necessarily fatal, but this case seems to me desperate. I need not tell you that I hope I am mistaken. Anyhow, you have Cottard, you're in excellent hands. Excuse me," he broke off as a maid came into the room with his coat over her arm. "I told you, I'm dining with the Minister of Commerce, and I have a call to pay first. Ah! Life is not all a bed of roses, as one is likely to think at your age."
>
> And he graciously offered me his hand. I had shut the door behind me, and a footman was showing us into the hall when we heard a loud shout of rage. The maid had forgotten

> to cut and hem the buttonhole for the decorations. This
> would take another ten minutes. The professor continued to
> storm while I stood on the landing gazing at my grand-
> mother for whom there was not the slightest hope. Each of
> us is indeed alone. We started for home [2:318].

The shortness of the sentences alone is a striking technique in Proust. The pages devoted to the grandmother's last days show, on the other hand, a fairly
ingenious use of her condition—not always so much
for a narrative in itself, but as a means of showing a
variety of characters' reactions in the same circumstances. It provides a shift of perspective on them.

At the beginning of *Guermantes* II-2, the narrative
does not simply pick up again after a period of mourn-
ing in the narrator's life. We know, because the fog
reminds the narrator of Doncières a year before, that
his grandmother has been dead for only a few months
at the very most, but a whole series of pluperfects
reveals that much has happened that we are unaware
of, some of it apparently even before Mme de
Villeparisis's *matinée*. This is one of Proust's extraordinary manipulations of time and perspective.

> It depressed me all the more that I should be spending this
> Sunday by myself because I had sent a note that morning to
> Mlle de Stermaria. Robert de Saint-Loup, whom his mother
> had at length succeeded in parting—after painful and abor-
> tive attempts—from his mistress, and who immediately af-
> terward had been sent to Morocco in the hope of his there
> forgetting one whom he had already for some little time
> ceased to love, had sent me a line. . . . He warned me to
> waste no time in writing to Mlle de Stermaria. . . . This had
> come as no surprise, although I had had no news of him
> since, at the time of my grandmother's last illness, he had
> accused me of perfidy and treachery [2:347–48].

At some point the narrator has stopped annoying
Mme de Guermantes with his attentions and now has
conceived the idea of seducing Mlle de Stermaria,

whom he had glimpsed at Balbec and whom Saint-Loup has seen in Morocco. The next few days are taken up with this project, which will turn out to be futile, and an unexpected invitation to dinner from the duchess of Guermantes will provide a new distraction to make up partially for it. The unforeseen appearances of Albertine and Saint-Loup and the changes in them will contribute to our reordered picture of the narrator's world of friends and occupations. Obviously the scenes with Albertine and Saint-Loup are germane to the general pattern in *À la recherche* of showing changes in character—and even a total reversal in the case of Saint-Loup—but what of Mlle de Stermaria? The narrator insists at the moment and much later that her role in *À la recherche* is to demonstrate negative chance.

> As for Albertine, I had no more doubt. I was sure that it could have been not Albertine that I loved, that it might have been some one else. To prove this, it would have been sufficient that Mlle de Stermaria, on the evening when I was to take her to dine on the island in the Bois, should not have put me off [3:501].

Mlle de Stermaria possesses the mystery that more than anything else attracts the narrator to women, and she appears in his imagination associated with her misty Breton chateau. It is pure coincidence that makes Albertine and not her the central figure in the narrator's sentimental life. We see in this fortuity, and in the fact that (unlike most women in her situation) the duchess of Guermantes has not been disgusted with him forever but decides he must be interesting, how large issues in the narrator's life are being decided before we know it.

Le Côté de Guermantes deals mainly with two social occasions flanking the personal event of the grand-

mother's death, and thus has in its large outline the
A B A pattern we have already noted. Because of its
predominantly social dimension, we do not expect
reflections on the narrator's more and more forgotten
vocation, but one significant juxtaposition does occur.
As he is going down the staircase with Saint-Loup and
setting off for a restaurant, the narrator has experiences of involuntary memory, which are contrasted
with the empty pleasures of society and friendship.
One thing that is important and sometimes overlooked
is that while the narrator has long known such experiences, there is not yet, as there was not for the boy in
Combray, any clear connection between literary creation and memories of that sort. He passes by the
experience of revelation like the pure fool Parsifal of
that favorite *Symbolist* quest myth. It has been said that
the final revelation of *Le Temps retrouvé* has been made
many times over throughout the novel, but it is only
the quality of involuntary memory that is observed,
not its role for fiction. The comparisons the narrator
makes between it and esthetic experiences remain
enigmatic to him.

Proust's use of digression or omniscient commentary can be seen as a kind of elaboration on the
details of the scene at hand, but discursiveness becomes altogether something else in the passage, about
fifty pages long, interposed between the entrance of
the Guermantes and their guests into the dining room
and the beginning of conservation at table (2:135 83).
This extraordinary piece of writing does not have really
comparable analogues in other novels; it is a combination of essay, portraits, summary narration, gossip,
and anecdote, all in a sustained brilliant, ironic style.
The intentionality governing this part of *Guermantes*
has been explained earlier as the narrator's conclusion,

after mythologizing the Guermantes and then finding them common, that they have a historical and social interest which, if limited, is genuine. The gap between a young, naive narrating voice and an older one has been closed. The narrator amply proves in this excursus that the Guermantes are far from the least rewarding family to observe. Proust was very conscious of the modern reader's reaction to Saint-Simon: he finds the memorialist's style is often superior to his subject and is perplexed by the silliness or flatness of the examples of seventeenth-century conversational wit given in the *Mémoires*. Proust attempts, by selection and concentration of epigrams, anecdotes, puns, and a running ironic commentary, to make the wit of his social comedy as perdurable as that of Molière.

The essay-portrait of the Guermantes is in proportion to the whole dinner episode itself, which is one of the most striking examples of temporal protraction in Proust. I have observed that certain minutes in *À la recherche* receive an enlargement and detail that makes reading about them at least as long as the minutes themselves. Much the same may be said of the dinner. Until Proust and Joyce, it was perhaps always true that, in respect to time, fiction miniaturized life; after them, the inverse relation existed. What is interesting about these prolongations of detailed action is that it takes a number of readings before any feeling of organization emerges from them, for they represent another aspect of Proust's indifference to neat, scenic technique.

In *Guermantes* I the main episodes were linked to seasons. Something peculiar happens in *Guermantes* II. Proust continues the seasonal linkage of events, but now time becomes accelerated according to a purely imaginative, stylized system. The week the narrator failed to seduce Mlle de Stermaria is in autumn; there is talk of snow as he leaves the duchess's dinner party, at the end of that very week, and two months later he receives an invitation from the princess of Guermantes for a party that takes place only in summer. Nor is this the last place where Proust sacrifices realistic chronology to obtain seasonal coloring in an episode or the heightened effect of foreshortening.

The other temporal juggling in *Guermantes* II is the movement, for a couple of pages, into an iterative summer party at the duchess's, after which we modulate back into winter and punctual time (2:512–14). The final scene, that with the Guermantes, the fatally ill Swann, and the narrator, leads into the time scheme of *Sodome et Gomorrhe*, but thematically it is very much part of the study of the duke and duchess. Like the narration of the grandmother's stroke, it belongs to conventional technique and constitutes a scene of the kind Flaubert would have understood. What commentary there is to be found is brief and free of digressions; dialogue constitutes most of the scene. The effect of this kind of narration is intensified by its rarity.

The durative tension of the long day that bridges *Le Côté de Guermantes* and *Sodome et Gomorrhe* is greater than what we have seen until now, since the narrator is worried about the genuineness of his invitation to the unknown princess of Guermantes's party, and then concerned about returning home in time for Albertine's late-evening visit. The quality of factitious worry is seen even in the rumors that the prince of Guermantes has been nasty to Swann, who has appeared at the party and is closeted briefly with him. (There is no disagreeable incident, however, and the different tone of their interview makes it the core of the thematic *A B A* pattern of the party.) The narrator's disquiet at being the possible object of an unpleasant scene is not, of course, out of proportion with the profoundly egocentric behavior of most of the characters on that day, including even Albertine, who is unwilling to sacrifice some pleasure to come calm him. In the last instance, the narrator himself is acting quite as self-seekingly as the other characters, and I have already noted the disagreeable new tone in his behavior with Albertine in *Sodome*. Here the nonomniscient narrator unknowingly foresees his future, with ironic tension for the reader.

> As I listened to these words of deprecation, uttered as though she did not intend to come, I felt that, with the longing to see that velvet-blooming face . . . a very different element was painfully endeavouring to combine. This terrible need of a person I had learned to know at Combray in the case of my mother. . . . I should never unravel the truth: and . . . it would always be so, unless I were to shut her [Albertine] up in prison (but prisoners escape) until the end. . . . I could detect a shuddering anticipation of long periods of suffering to come [2:733-34].

Much of *Sodome* will consist of attempts to still anguish and ward off the inevitable consequences of psychological determinism. The passage I have just quoted is designed, in connection with the short final chapter, to make of *Sodome* an elegant cycle, with apprehensions of his future life with Albertine at beginning and end.

Something curious occurs in the commentary on persons during the princess's party and immediately after: a future dimension to their social lives begins to open, and the narrator speaks especially of the decline of the Guermantes, and notably of Charlus, after this last great appearance in society. It has only been a few months since the haughty grandeurs of the duchess's dinner party, and there is a sudden acceleration of the inevitable process of change. In the short "summer visits" postlude to the princess's *soirée*, we see the new positions in the world occupied by Odette's and Mme Verdurin's salons, and the narrator, having exhausted the interest the Guermantes have for him, is investigating various less well-known areas of society. What is technically striking about this short coda is that time in it is completely blurred; enormous changes are taking place, but we cannot say exactly when. Such vague temporality has not occurred in the novel since "Un Amour de Swann," and it contrasts especially with the continuous chronology that has obtained since the beginning of *Guermantes*.

The temporality of the pages devoted to changes in society and opening onto the future is blurred but not in the least relaxed; Proust manages paradoxically to make us feel movement without points of reference. The rest of *Sodome* II-1, the Balbec section, and II-2 as well, contain many of the "one day" kinds of time indications but have an almost achronic quality. We feel a shift in narrative method from the preceding account of the retrospectively "degrading" social life. The most surprising thing, however, is that between the summer visits and the spring in Balbec there is no intervening material or explicit lapse of time alluded to, and, of course, this corresponds to nothing else in the central narrative of *À la recherche*. The reason for the leap in time is not completely elusive, however. The intermittencies of the heart, of the narrator's memory of his grandmother, are the subject, and the spring weather and flowering apple tree present us with a Combray complex of associations. The race of Combray and its characteristic imagery are evoked between the manifestations of Sodom.

There is a grotesque element of intentionality in the visit to Balbec: the narrator is expecting to meet Baroness Putbus and her chambermaid, about whom Saint-Loup has had much to say. In the meantime, days pass—there are about eighteen such time indications—and while nascent suspicions about Albertine's sexual preferences occasionally disturb the narrator deeply, they never form the kind of causal and chronological chain which would result in sustained tension. After the high season begins, much of *Sodome* will be devoted to a period when the narrator is relatively free of worries about Albertine and feels little urgency in his life. For the novelist this presents quite a problem, since connection and a somehow meaningful sequence are indispensable to his art. Proust's initial solution is to create another couple, Charlus and Morel, who will absorb some of the reader's attention, and to organize the summer partly around a place and a ceremony—the Verdurins' Wednesday evening dinners.

The first of these, which involves a train trip taken as a group by nearly all the faithful, occupies much of *Sodome* II-2 and moves in chapter 3 to an early autumn typical-imperfect Verdurin evening. The later part of chapter 3 will be devoted to a brilliant invention: the train trip to and from the dinner is recounted in a mixed imperfect-preterite mode, Charlus's reading a volume of Balzac being the unifying motif; the dinner itself, however, is omitted. The train stations bring to mind anecdotes, often of coincidences. All these mechanics of social life render the repetitious emptiness of the summer, but it is an emptiness that is willed, since for the narrator the alternative is more freedom for Albertine to prowl about on her own and excite his anguish. Between the punctual dinner in chapter 2 and the train circuit in chapter 3, there are anecdotes about the other couple and, inevitably, the account of the narrator and Albertine's days. The extensive social life the narrator leads (2:1022) is omitted, and the typical-iterative days with Albertine, in which the cycle of anguish and calm is repeated, occupy our attention.

Chapter 3 introduces a new device for creating tension: the narrator refers to what he will learn later, especially about their chauffeur.

> What unfortunately I did not know at that moment and did not learn until more than two years later was that one of the chauffeur's patrons was M. de Charlus, and that Morel, instructed to pay him and keeping part of the money for himself (making the chauffeur triple and quintuple the mileage), had become very friendly with him (while pretending not to know him before other people) and made use of his car for long journeys. If I had known this at the time, and that the confidence which the Verdurins were presently to feel in this chauffeur came, unknown to them, from that source, perhaps many of the sorrows of my life in Paris, in the year that followed, much of my trouble over Albertine would have been avoided, but I had not the slightest suspicion of it [2:1006; cf. 2:1031–32].

In this way the center of *Sodome*, devoted to disconnected episodes and stories of coincidences, can point toward an end (the desire to see Mme Putbus's chambermaid has long since disappeared). The form action and temporality assume in most of *Sodome*, however, is not to be judged by itself (in which case the anticipations might seem like a rather naive plot device), but rather in relation to the technique of *La Prisonnière*, or even to the last, short chapter of *Sodome*, in which the revelations about Albertine's past have an intensely dramatic and punctual character after the many gently monotonous imperfects. The sustained, simultaneous feeling of causal enchainment and temporal urgency in that last chapter is what we have not felt since the Balbec episode began months before.

The opening day of *La Prisonnière* is a perfect example of the typical aspect in narrative; Proust even calls it a "matinée idéale." It and the agitated day which comprises the largest part of *La Prisonnière* represent calm and anguish, the two moods the narrator has recognized as dominating him since an early period of his stay in Balbec. At one point the imperfect tenses yield to a largely preterite call paid on the duchess of Guermantes. The *A B A* situations, private-public-private, are reinforced by change of aspect.

There are a few briefly recounted days before and after the long major one of *La Prisonnière*, showing Proust's usual fondness for somewhat blurred preludes and endings to units of time. We must always bear in mind the analogy with the soft-edged quality of memories which Proust seems to be aiming at. Aside from the interplay of themes in the more reflective passages of that preeminent day, its most salient part is the narrator's attendance at the party given by Charlus and the Verdurins to make Morel and his gifts known to society. There are two striking ways of accelerating time here. First, Charlus, suddenly seeming much older, is trailed by *apaches* in the street before the party. "Making a pretence of not seeing the seedy individual who was following in his wake (whenever the baron ventured on the boulevards or crossed the waiting room at the Gare Saint-Lazare, these followers might be counted by the dozen who, in the hope of 'touching him for a dollar,' never let him out of their sight), and afraid at the same time that the other might have the audacity to accost him, the baron had devoutly lowered his darkened eyelids which, in contrast to his rice-powdered cheeks, gave him the appearance of a Grand Inquisitor painted by El Greco" (3:207). It is less than six months since his appearances in Balbec, when no such suspect entourage was attached to his person (3:204, 212). Then, listening to the Vinteuil septet, the narrator realizes what an elaborate concatenation of circumstances was necessary for that particular piece of music to be played in that particular house on that evening. From the vision of punishment and fate at the end of *Sodome* through to the end, each part of *À la recherche* will have its own scene where the narrator realizes the surprises and ironies of causality in his life: these plunge him into the feeling of time as well, and give him the sense of aging. The party itself, the center of an *A B A* arrangement of the day, concludes with an extraordinary scene in which for once the dramatic analogy of "scene" is fully appropriate; the small cast, well-defined setting, sharply delineated speeches, gestures, entrances, and exits all are there.

As a part of the regular rhythm of calm and anguish, *La Prisonnière* concludes with spring weather accompanied by thoughts of Venice and leaving Albertine. After the latter's departure at the end, *La Fugitive* continues the seasonal cycle, though with little of the imagistic immediacy of early parts of *À la recherche*. As the summer spanning *La Fugitive* and *Le Temps retrouvé* in our editions begins, we have a last example of accelerating time. Gilberte and Saint-Loup are barely married by the measure of realistic time when their disunion seems of long standing.

Aside from the war episode, where two different visits to Paris are told in Proust's interweaving manner, the later parts of *À la recherche*, from Albertine's departure until the princess of Guermantes's *matinée*, do not attempt to convey the passage of time so vividly. The stages the narrator perceives in forgetting

Albertine are not experienced as positive states, but as emptiness. The marriages between aristocrats and commoners, which would have so shocked the grandmother, are described as merely surprising facts; they are not dramatically conveyed. In the same way, Gilberte's conversations about the past with the narrator are merely dry recountings of what once happened. The narrator's mind is no longer so rich in imagery, and since the present is uniform in color, it calls up no analogies with the past. The narrator and reader experience this phase of his life as achronic. It is for this reason that the conclusion of the novel is double, a feature of it not always understood, since the narrator's decision to enter the princess's grand salon and see the guests "got up as old people" does not seem necessarily to follow from his meditation in the library on involuntary memory. Yet there really must be some sense of time's passage if we are fully to understand involuntary memory as a link between past and present. In a featureless achronism there would be little impetus for the deflagration of memory, as Proust had earlier illustrated it. At the same time, we must bear in mind that the last sight of the characters in the disguise of old age in no way bespeaks the "philosophical *vanitas*," or lament for the past, traditional in literature.

During the narrator's session of sweet silent thought in the library, and at the very end of *Le Temps retrouvé*, the *drame du coucher* is very present in his mind, so that instead of a dénouement and complete undoing of narrative tension, we are referred back to the beginning of the novel. This is a one-time cycle, as opposed to the endlessly iterative activity of the profane world of history and society. But the most interesting fact about the cyclic pattern is not the repetition, but the aspect of tension I have alluded to; the moments of relaxed temporality and causal relations are within the formal body, not antecedent and posterior to it. Ultimately, all the questions of time and cause we have been examining combine to create tensional patterns, which are the underlying basis of narration. Proust's plotting out of his novel has the interesting characteristic that he avoids the commonest ways of forming these patterns, like the large and obvious concatenation of events or providing the main character with a problem of one kind or another, the working out of which sustains interest and gives the impression of unity.

In the absence of a steady movement toward some end, however, Proust does employ certain devices of traditional fiction. "Preparation" is one, and we see it, for example, in the fact that elements of the baron-Jupien scene are brought in much earlier, such as the rare flower and the empty basement. There are also enigmas eventually solved: the identity of the lady in pink or of the young man with whom Gilberte was walking in the street. The preparation and enigmas are very close to the kind of causal relations, such as coincidences, Proust likes, in that they are presented in small segments. He is especially fond of the contrast between apparent freedom or miscellaneousness of events and secret, minute relations. Here the narrator thinks of his "indispensable" life with Albertine:

> Indispensable without perhaps having been in itself and at the outset a thing that was necessary, since I should not have known Albertine had I not read in an archeological treatise a description of the church at Balbec, had not Swann, by telling me that this church was almost Persian, directed my taste to the Byzantine Norman, had not a financial syndicate, by erecting at Balbec a hygienic and comfortable hotel, made my parents decide to hear my supplication and send me to

Balbec. . . . Who would have told me at Combray when I lay
waiting for my mother's goodnight with so heavy a heart,
that those anxieties would be healed, and would then break
out again one day for a girl who would at first be no more
. . . than a flower upon which my eyes would . . . be invited
to gaze [3:500–501].

Enigmas and causes join at times, as when the narrator
learns to his surprise that Norpois has spoken favor-
ably of him to the duchess of Guermantes. The effect of
unexpected concatenations of incidents is not, of
course, unfamiliar in more traditional fiction, but
Proust has a completely idiosyncratic way of balancing
such enchainments with temporal dilution, reversal,
acceleration, and so forth, so that our immediate perception of them is fitful.

The effects I have just been discussing would
seem to bring about some dispersal of the reader's
attention, to distract him from the larger movement of
the novel by sporadic episodes of causal enchainment
or unexpected satisfactions of curiosity. Indeed, the
close examination of temporal patterns might seem to
persuade us that cause and time are highly fragmented
in *À la recherche*. Working toward unity of effect, however, is a large-scale organization of time.

One of the most successful and ingenious aspects
of the creation of fictional time in Proust's novel concerns the grouping of events into large regions of
memory or periods, each with a coloring derived from
aspects of life which bear only indirectly on the plot.
Thus the early days, of which the narrator has in part
but heard, are the time of bustles and bric-a-brac,
Odette's chinoiseries and the *jardin d'hiver*. "I was in
bed with her the day MacMahon resigned," remarks a
man in the crowd admiring Odette in the Bois. The
event alluded to took place in November 1879 (and

Odette had been young during the *Septennat*, the early Third Republic). Swann is invited to lunch at the Élysée by Grévy, president from 1879 to 1887. No one yet uses the telephone and electric lights are uncommon. At the end of this period Louis XVI and white walls come into style, the Far East retreating before the eighteenth century in Odette's drawing room. Fashion and technology, even more than political life, give us the feeling of a distant past, and the unspecified lapse of time after *À l'ombre* defines its events, along with those in *Swann*, as the days of childhood and adolescence.

Instead of characterizing the time of the narrator's entrance into society merely with more changes in clothes and interior decoration, Proust makes it coincide with a very well-defined and important series of events in French life, the Dreyfus case. The narrator is in Doncières in autumn (*Le Côté de Guermantes* I), and the case exploded in November 1897 with the publication by Dreyfus's brother of the forged document on which the conviction rested. Zola's open letter ("J'accuse," January 1898) and his trial (February 1898) followed, and the spring of Mme de Villeparisis's reception is that of the petitions or *listes révisionnistes*. The last phase of the case, the second trial, coincides with the princess of Guermantes's party (June 1899). Throughout all this, of course, the characters have been talking abundantly about these events. Thereafter the "days of the *Affaire*" are referred to as ancient history, a break in precise chronology occurring at just that point in the novel (*Sodome et Gomorrhe* II-1).

In the third period of the novel, that of Albertine and the consequences of the narrator's monstrous attachment to her, technology lends its note to life. The telephone has been growing in acceptance and usefulness, and now automobiles, airplanes, and cinema begin to play a role. Modern music (Vinteuil) is better known, the Ballets Russes appear in Paris, and Andrée's fiancé practices the new style of stage design, after the examples of Adolphe Appia or Gordon Craig, so that we feel the presence of the avant-garde which characterized artistic life in the years immediately preceding the outbreak of World War I. (There are of course many significant movements in art and literature which are not mentioned; one suspects Proust's taste was basically rather conservative.)

These correlations between real time and events and fiction are handled with great delicacy and, in particular, leave the earliest and latest parts of *A la recherche* in an indeterminate zone, so we do not have the feeling of a framed narrative, beginning in such and such a year and ending with equal precision. Even in the central section, dates are always avoided; Proust's aim is not to prove that he is following a real or plausible chronology, but rather to endow the reader with a kind of fictional memory, analogous to that which a middle-aged or older person would have in life, so that the reader may look back with the narrator and distinguish, as the latter does, periods suffused with a certain emotive color. We recall, as part of our acquired fictional experience, the expectations and the charm of myth in childhood and adolescence, fascination with the realities of life among people unconstrained by practical cares of money or professional ambition, and, finally, the love affair toward which the narrator had been unconsciously impelled by the whole "disastrous way" his "psychopathological mechanism" functioned.

My discussion of questions of time, intentionality, and causal relations has necessarily been rather abstract. I have, indeed, quoted some passages involving verb tenses, dense visual imagery, and unusually short sentences when it seemed easier to illustrate a technique than simply to describe it, but if we were merely to imagine Proust's novel from a description of the relationships between events in it, we might conceive of it as a somewhat dry experiment in technique, like certain recent novels that in many ways present themselves as puzzles and appeal to a somewhat different taste and type of reading from the traditional novel. The fact is, however, that Proust's dominant concern as an artist was for a continuity of style in which all his exceptional techniques would be absorbed, so as to produce a total, unified vision. This is the final, highest level of artistic consideration we must deal with in Proust's novel, and I hope to show how the process of absorption of individual techniques results in an integrated, seamless verbal medium.

3

the verbal texture

Chateaubriand, especially in his *Mémoires d'outre-tombe*, was one of the great models of heightened style in Proust's youth. He had, at an early point in his career, introduced a luxuriance of imagery into French prose unknown up to then, but the basis of his more elaborate sentences involves other elements as well.

> Recontrais-je quelque laboureur au bout d'un guéret? je m'arrêtais pour regarder cet homme germé à l'ombre des épis parmi lesquels il devait être moissonné, et qui retournant la terre de sa tombe avec le soc de la charrue, mêlait ses sueurs brûlantes aux pluies glacées de l'automne: le sillon qu'il creusait était le monument destinée à lui survivre [*Mémoires*, 1, 3:13].

> [And if I encountered some ploughsman at the end of his field? I stopped to look at this man sprouted in the shadow of the wheat stalks where he was to be harvested, turning the earth of his grave with the ploughshare, and mingling his burning sweat with the icy rains of autumn: the furrow he was digging was the monument destined to outlast him.]

94

If we examine the prose carefully, we see that many rhythmic phrases in juxtaposition have the same or almost the same length. The whole can be represented thus in respect to number of syllables per phrase: 9 / 5? / 4 / 6 / 4 / 4 / 4 / 4, / 2 / 8 / 8, / 7 / 7: / 6 / 6 / 7. The technical term for identical phrase groups is "isocolon," and along with antithesis, such as we find it in the last five phrases, isocolon belongs to the oldest known theory of artistic prose, that named for the sophist Gorgias, a contemporary of Plato. Gorgian rhetoric has, as its third constituent, the conscious play of sounds, and, although the form it takes in the quoted passage is too elusive for easy analysis, we may be sure that Chateaubriand had carefully tested his sentences for elegant vowel and consonant harmonies.

There is a further aspect to the structuring of French prose, and that is the handling of the last syllables of the sentence. Various effects are possible with the *chute de phrase*; one which is especially associated with Chateaubriand's practice is the placing of two relatively long (six to eight syllables) isocolonic units at the end of a sentence, as in our example: "mêlait . . . automne." The tripartite, near isocolonic pattern ("le sillon . . . survivre") is a variation. Often these phrases make up an alexandrine (6 / 6), which, while theoretically forbidden in prose since the advent of neoclassical esthetics, is actually a not uncommon rhythm in such circumstances. *Sodome* closes with the words, "Il faut absolument / que j'épouse Albertine." This sentence also shows that while we associate the isocolonic effect with impressive images, any material may be used. However, the concluding words of *À l'ombre* are more in keeping with usual practice. Françoise's opening the curtain to the sun is compared to the unwrapping of a mummy: "avant de la faire apparaitre, embaumée dans sa rob*e* d'or.'' In these examples we see Proust following Chateaubriand as far as near or complete isocolon, but without antithesis. When we have read a great deal of Proust's prose carefully and then turn to Chateaubriand's, we become aware how close the latter often is to over twenty centuries of rhetorical theory and practice and how far Proust has strayed from this tradition. He takes from it what he will, rather than adhering to it. This becomes especially evident when we examine a passage where Proust assumes the oratorical tone.

The longest sustained syntactic structure in Proust's novel, and one of the most grandiose in manner, is to be found in the sermon on the men-women of Sodom which takes up much of *Sodome* I. It begins:

> Il appartenait à la race de ces êtres, moins contradictoires qu'ils n'en ont l'air, dont l'idéal est viril, justement parce que leur tempérament est féminin, et qui sont dans la vie pareils, en apparence seulement, aux autres hommes; là où chacun porte, inscrite en ces yeux à travers lesquels il voit toutes choses dans l'univers, une silhouette intaillée dans la facette de la prunelle, pour eux ce n'est pas celle d'une nymphe, mais d'un éphèbe. Race sur qui pèse une malédiction et qui doit vivre dans le mensonge et le parjure, puisqu'elle sait tenu pour punissable et honteux, pour inavouable, son désir, ce qui fait pour toute créature la plus grande douceur de vivre; qui doit renier son Dieu, puisque, même chrétiens, quand à la barre du tribunal ils comparaissent comme accusés, il leur faut, devant le Christ et en son nom, se défendre comme d'une calomnie de ce qui est leur vie même; fils sans mère [2:614–15].

> [He belonged to that race of beings, less paradoxical than they appear, whose ideal is manly simply because their temperament is feminine and who in life resemble in appearance only the rest of men; there where each of us carries, inscribed in those eyes through which he beholds everything in the universe, a human outline engraved on the surface of the pupil, for them it is not that of a nymph but of a youth. Race

upon which a curse weighs and which must live amid falsehood and perjury, because it knows the world to regard as a
punishable and a scandalous, as an inadmissible thing, its
desire, that which constitutes for every human creature the
greatest happiness in life; which must deny its God, since
even if Christians, when at the bar of justice they appear and
are arraigned, they must before Christ and in His Name
defend themselves, as from a calumny, from the charge of
what to them is life itself; sons without a mother.]

Here the thought is constantly antithetical and some
isocolon does occur, but the two devices do not come
together in the showy manner of Chateaubriand; the
antitheses are not *pointed*. Proust's more or less conscious model was probably Jacques-Bénigne Bossuet,
who was relatively subtle in his handling of rhetoric
and who largely avoided the monotonous effect of
some seventeenth-century prose writers given to isocolon and antithesis. Even in his use of maxims,
another strongly neoclassical element in his style,
Proust tended to avoid the violently antithetical or the
overly epigrammatic.

In the use of irregular phrase lengths, however,
one further distinction must be made about Proust's
style. We find little in it like Flaubert's practice in this
passage from Part I, chapter 9 of *Madame Bovary*:

La nouvelle bonne obéissait sans murmure pour n'être point
renvoyée; et, comme Madame, d'habitude, laissait la clef au
buffet, Félicité, chaque soir, prenait une petite provision de
sucre qu'elle mangeait toute seule, dans son lit, après avoir
fait sa prière.

[The new maid obeyed without complaining for fear of being
dismissed; and, as Madame usually left the key on the side-
board, Félicité, each evening, took a little supply of sugar,
which she ate by herself in bed, after saying her prayers.]

The abnormally tiny rhythmic segments (produced

twice by distorting normal word order and placing an adverb between subject and verb) were Flaubert's way of avoiding the *style coulant* he detested and creating a sculptural, sharply defined sequence of phrases. He declaimed his prose as a test, and the effect was a new one in the history of French prose rhythm, one which influenced subsequent novelists. One objection to this kind of elaborately segmented phrasing is that it confers far too much grandeur on the quotidian; a counterobjection might be that the maid's stealing sugar is an important element of satisfaction in her otherwise barren life.

While some of the elegance of Flaubert's multiple pauses can be seen in passages where Proust aligns several verbs, nouns, or adjectives, the general effect of his numerous grammatical breaks and intercalations is quite different.

> Et aujourd'hui encore si, dans une grande ville de province ou dans un quartier de Paris que je connais mal, un passant qui m'a "mis dans mon chemin" me montre au loin, comme un point de repère, tel beffroi d'hôpital, tel clocher de couvent levant la pointe de son bonnet ecclésiastique au coin d'une rue que je dois prendre, pour peu que ma mémoire puisse obscurément lui trouver quelque trait de ressemblance avec la figure chère et disparue, le passant, s'il se retourne pour s'assurer que je ne m'égare pas, peut, à son étonnement, m'apercevoir qui, oublieux de la promenade entreprise ou de la course obligée, reste là, devant le clocher, pendant des heures, immobile, essayant de me souvenir, sentant au fond de moi des terres reconquises sur l'oubli qui s'assèchent et se rebâtissent; et sans doute alors, et plus anxieusement que tout à l'heure quand je lui demandais de me renseigner, je cherche encore mon chemin, je tourne une rue... mais... c'est dans mon coeur... [1:67]

> [And so even today in any large provincial town, or in a quarter of Paris which I do not know well, if a passerby who is "putting me on the right road" shows me from afar, as a point to aim at, some belfry of a hospital or a convent steeple

lifting the peak of its ecclesiastical cap at the corner of the
street which I am to take, my memory need only find in it
some dim resemblance to that dear and vanished outline,
and the passerby, should he turn round to make sure that I
have not gone astray, would see me, to his astonishment,
oblivious of the walk I had planned to take or the place where
I was obliged to call, standing still on the spot, before that
steeple, for hours on end, motionless, trying to remember,
feeling deep within myself a tract of soil reclaimed from the
waters of Lethe slowly drying until the buildings rise on it
again; and then no doubt, and then more uneasily than
when, just now, I asked him a for a direction, I will seek my
way again, I will turn a corner . . . but . . . the goal is in my
heart.]

Proust used punctuation very sparingly, unlike Flaubert, and editors have supplied the minimum necessary. It would be virtually impossible, in any case, to
divide the sentence into such small units as Flaubert
often uses, both because of the wording and because
Proust's relatively long sentences would disintegrate
under such subdivision. His rhythmic groups are
much closer to those of speech, and indeed the whole
passage has a colloquial feeling, like the speech of
someone enormously fluent and perfectly possessed
of grammar. One might compare a similar kind of
sentence in Henry James's late style, when he used
dictation, in this case from *The Wings of the Dove.*

Merton Densher, who passed the best hours of each night at
the office of his newspaper, had at times, during the day, to
make up for it, a sense, or at least an appearance, of leisure,
in accordance with which he was frequently to be met, in
different parts of the town, at moments when men of busi-
ness are hidden from the public eye.

The same effect of brilliant improvisation is there. Actually, I am obliged to observe that, despite the fact
that long sentences are often associated with formal
rhetoric and oratory, as in the quotation above from

Sodome I (2:614–15), only limited amounts of parenthetical or grammatically subordinated material can be
accommodated in such styles. Beyond a certain degree
of elaboration, the declamatory force is broken: it has
often been observed that Proust's most difficult sentences become syntactically transparent when read
aloud, but that means in a middle tone, free from the
manner of public delivery. Thus Proust's prose differs
markedly from the oratorical tradition of high style in
French. I have explored further these questions of
Proust's style and previous prose in *The Traditions of
French Prose Style: A Rhetorical Study* (Baton Rouge:
Louisiana State University Press, 1981).

There are certain elements of prose style which
cut across the distinctions of tone I have noted and
bring us to the very heart of Proust's feeling for language. Looking closely at the relatively informal passage above ("Et aujourd'hui . . . "), one may perceive
six places where a particular construction or part of
speech occurs in pairs. Such doublings were not part
of the Gorgian theory of style, though they were frequent in such classical writers as Cicero. In French the
elaboration of style has depended to a large extent on
this practice since the Middle French humanists; doubling is, in some ways, the major symmetrical figure.
The essay style lends itself particularly to doublings, as
in the following.

> Pendant ces périodes où, tout en s'affaiblissant, persiste
> le chagrin, il faut distinguer entre celui que nous cause la
> pensée constante de la personne elle-même, et celui que
> raniment certains souvenirs, telle phrase méchante dite, tel
> verbe employé dans une lettre qu'on a reçue. En réservant de
> décrire, à l'occasion d'un amour ultérieur, les formes di-
> verses du chagrin, disons que, de ces deux-là, la première est
> infiniment moins cruelle que la seconde. Cela tient à ce que
> notre notion de la personne, vivant toujours en nous, y est

embellie de l'auréole que nous ne tardons pas à lui rendre, et s'emprint sinon des douceurs fréquentes de l'espoir, tout au moins du calme d'une tristesse permanente [1:627].

[During those periods in which our bitterness of spirit, though steadily diminishing, still persists, a distinction must be drawn between the bitterness which comes to us from our constantly thinking of the person herself and that which is revived by certain memories, some cutting speech, some word in a letter that we have had from her. The various forms which that bitterness can assume we shall examine when we come to deal with another and later love affair; for the present it must suffice to say that, of these two kinds, the former is infinitely the less cruel. That is because our conception of the person, since it dwells always within ourselves, is there adorned with the halo with which we are bound before long to invest her, and bears the marks if not of the frequent solace of hope, at any rate of the tranquility of a permanent sorrow.]

The first doubling, with antithesis, involves an element of variety: a participle, "s'affaiblissant," matches a finite verb form, "persiste." The "celui" doubling needs no comment, but it should be noted that "telle . . . tel . . . " is merely a form of the pattern *A* or *B* with the conjunction omitted. An antithesis follows, and two finite verbs in *em-* come next, followed by the balancing nouns and adverbs "sinon . . . au moins." However, the pronounced binary symmetries of the quoted passage yield to more varied patterns in the sentences which follow it.

Mais si l'idée de la personne que nous aimons reçoit la reflet d'une intelligence généralement optimiste, il n'en est pas de même des souvenirs particuliers, de ces propos méchants, de cette lettre hostile (je n'en reçus qu'une seule qui le fût, de Gilberte), on dirait que la personne elle-même réside dans ces fragments pourtant si restreints, et portée à une puissance qu'elle est bien loin d'avoir dans l'idée habituelle que nous nous formons d'elle tout entière. C'est que la lettre, nous ne l'avons pas, comme l'image de l'être aimé, contemplée dans le calme mélancolique du regret; nous l'avons

lue, dévorée, dans l'angoisse affreuse dont nous étreignait
un malheur inattendu.

[But if the idea of the person whom we love catches and
reflects a ray of light from a mind which is on the whole
optimistic, it is not so with those special memories, those
cutting words, that inimical letter (I received only one that
could be so described from Gilberte); you would say that the
person herself dwelt in those fragments, few and scattered as
they are and dwelt there multiplied to a power of which she
falls ever so far short in the idea which we are accustomed to
form of her as a whole. Because the letter has not—as the
image of the beloved creature has—been contemplated by us
in the melancholy calm of regret; we have read it, devoured it
in the fearful anguish with which we were wrung by an
unforeseen misfortune.]

"If" clauses with their conclusion often form a balancing pair and even an antithetical one, as here.
"Souvenirs," "propos," and "lettre" may seem irregu-
larly constructed, but *A, B, C* rather than *A, B,* and *C* is
common in Latin and occurs as a formal alternative in
all periods of French prose beginning with the Renais-
sance. The parallelism of "réside" and "portée" ("est
portée") is elliptical, and a further irregularity occurs in
the use of the absolute noun, "la lettre," which is
caught up by a reprise object pronoun. In the middle of
the final antithesis occurs a significant example of
asyndeton: "lue," "dévorée." The *A, B* formula here is
not merely the equivalent of "lue et dévorée," which
gives a solidity and finality Proust does not want, but
serves rather to give a reflective, self-correcting, and
refining nuance. This is one of Proust's favorite constructions, rare in most great French prose stylists
before Flaubert and capable of great suggestiveness.

As I have cited examples of the basic parallelism
to which many—perhaps even most—prose writers
tend, we have eventually encountered some irregu-

larities. These asymmetric elements constitute enormously important variables in Proust's style, which owes its remarkable richness and flexibility to precisely this possibility of countering balancing patterns with asymmetry of different kinds and degrees, a subject first broached in Bernd Spillner's *Symmetriches und asymmetriches Prinzip in der Syntax Marcel Prousts* (Meisenheim-am-Glan: Hain, 1971). I am going to examine a variety of passages illustrating types of asymmetry, noting, as they occur, certain other devices to which I shall ultimately return. The following is an excellent example of the interplay of regularity and asymmetry.

> Elle disait: "Enfin, on respire!" et parcourait les allées détrempées—trop symétriquement alignées à son gré par le nouveau jardinier dépourvu du sentiment de la nature et auquel mon père avait demandé depuis le matin si le temps s'arrangerait—de son petit pas enthousiaste et saccadé, réglé sur les mouvements divers qu'excitaient dans son âme l'ivresse de l'orage, la puissance de l'hygiène, la stupidité de mon éducation et la symétrie des jardins, plutôt que sur le désir inconnu d'elle, d'éviter à sa jupe prune les taches de boue sous lesquelles elle disparaissait jusqu'à une hauteur qui était toujours pour sa femme de chambre un désespoir et un problème [1:11].

> [She would say, "At last one can breathe!" and would run up and down the soaking paths—too straight and symmetrical for her liking, owing to the want of any feeling for nature in the new gardener, whom my father had been asking all morning if the weather were going to clear up—with her keen, jerky little step regulated by the various effects wrought upon her soul by the intoxication of the storm, the force of hygiene, the stupidity of the way I was being raised, and symmetry in gardens, rather than by any anxiety (for that was quite unknown to her) to save her plum-colored skirt from the spots of mud under which it would gradually disappear to a depth which always provided her maid with a fresh problem and filled her with fresh despair.]

The overall sentence shape demonstrates a basic stylistic resource. Many sentences can be divided, for practical purposes, into a subject unit, a verb unit, and complementary material following the verb; the balance or imbalance of these three parts determines the kind of movement the sentence has, within itself and in relation to context. Here, of course, the complement is everything, and we feel the whole has a mildly associative, casual progress. (I should note in passing the problem of wholeness of sense: the "auquel" clause and the last "qui" clause do not show that logical connection, specific or implied, with the main clause which is normally expected of subordinate constructions.) On the other hand, a certain solidity and feeling of definition is conferred on the whole structure by the four *A* and *B* patterns of nouns or modifiers and by the firm *A, B, C,* and *D* gait of the four nouns in succession. But again, if we observe the doublings more closely, we see that "dépourvu" and "auquel," besides having no parallel or antithetical sense, are grammatically dissimilar and belong to a type of pseudosymmetry condemned by grammarians. As a general conclusion, one may say that equilibrating patterns here are free from the mechanical effect they often have in essayistic styles and recapture some of their original architectural grandeur.

The next example has firmness and even pomp in its many regular doublings and triplings (*A* and *B, A* or *B, A, B, C,* and *A, B,* and *C*).

> Tandis que dans cet escalier pestilentiel et désiré de l'ancienne couturière, comme il n'y en avait pas un second pour le service, on voyait le soir devant chaque porte une boîte au lait vide et sale préparée sur le paillasson, dans l'escalier magnifique et dédaigné que Swann montait à ce moment, d'un côté et de l'autre, à des hauteurs différentes,

devant chaque anfractuosité que faisait dans le mur la fenêtre
de la loge ou la porte d'un appartement, représentant le
service intérieur qu'ils dirigeaient et en faisant hommage aux
invités, un concierge, un majordome, un argentier (braves
gens qui vivaient le reste de la semaine un peu indépendants
dans leur domaine, y dinaient chez eux comme de petits
boutiquiers et seraient peut-être demain au service bour-
geois d'un médecin ou d'un industriel), attentifs à ne pas
manquer aux recommandations qu'on leur avait faites avant
de leur laisser endosser la livrée éclatante qu'ils ne revêtaient
qu'à de rares intervalles et dans laquelle ils ne se sentaient
pas très à leur aise, se tenaient sous l'arcature de leur portail
avec un éclat pompeux tempéré de bonhomie populaire,
comme des saints dans leur niche; et un énorme suisse,
habillé comme à l'église, frappait les dalles de sa canne au
passage de chaque arrivant [1:325].

[Whereas upon that pestilential, enviable staircase to the old
dressmaker's, since there was no other, no service stair in the
building, one saw in the evening outside every door an
empty, unwashed milk can set out, in readiness for the
morning round, upon the doormat; on the despicable, enormous staircase which Swann was at that moment climbing,
on either side of him at different levels, before each anfrac-
tuosity made in its walls by the window of the porter's lodge
or the entrance to a set of rooms, representing the depart-
ments of indoor service which they controlled, and doing
homage for them to the guests, a concierge, a majordomo, a
steward (worthy men who spent the rest of the week in
semi-independence in their own domains, dined there by
themselves like small shopkeepers, and might tomorrow
lapse to the plebeian service of some successful doctor or
industrial magnate), scrupulous in carrying out to the letter
all the instructions that had been heaped upon them before
they were allowed to don the brilliant livery which they wore
only at long intervals, and in which they did not feel altogether at their ease, stood each in the arcade of his doorway,
their splendid pomp tempered by a democratic good-
fellowship, like saints in their niches; and a gigantic usher,
dressed Swiss Guard fashion, like the beadle in a church,
struck the pavement with his staff as each fresh arrival
passed him.]

The larger structure is, of course, a compound sentence in which the second part ("et un énorme suisse . . . ") is completely out of proportion to the first; a more normal construction would be to subordinate it with a "pendant que" or something of the sort. However, the feeling of extreme irregularity that the parallel compound structure gives isolates and draws attention to the last details, which might otherwise pass almost unnoticed.

Within the first part of the compound sentence an equal disproportion occurs. Half of it is given over to modifiers preceding the subject, and almost as much to the subject ("un concierge," "un majordome," "un argentier") and its postpositional modifiers, so that there is only a very modest verb and complement—modest in both sense and length—at the end. The great mass of modifiers before the subject is not difficult to analyze. While it is common enough to begin a sentence with one adverbial clause, one prepositional phrase, or one participle, here Proust uses all these constructions and, moreover, multiplies each one. The irregularity is one of profusion, as is often the case in his prose; he oversteps what has probably never been formulated as a grammatical rule, but is only a stylistic habit. Incidentally, one of the characteristic signs of Proust's syntax, which is rare or inexistent in other writers, is the double initial adverbial clause. Only in a few set constructions is this normally used in French ("quand il sera venu et que je l'aurai vu"; "s'il vient et que je le voie"). In Proust the unaccustomed second, uncoordinated adverbial clause gives the impression not so much of formality as of elaborate reasoning, of parenthetical precision.

We have previously seen the effect of a sentence in which the verbal complement preponderates; in lieu of tautness and suspension it offers unforeseen grammatical turns and accessory details. Here, on the other hand, we have a process of methodically building up a total image before the verb; we always know that ahead of us lies the subject, then the verb, then the verbal complement. The asymmetry of this sentence has perhaps less poetry, but it displays, as the earlier example did not, a conception of the elaborate sentence closer to the period of classical rhetorical theory, in that the tension is maintained through to the verb, which occupies the end position or near end position in both Proust's structure and in Latin prose. This asymmetry, then, with its syntactic suspense, is of a quite different order, and the use of balancing figures simply reinforces the magniloquent periodic movement. At the same time, we must note that a latinizing period such as this is rare in other French prose stylists after the sixteenth century; neoclassical notions of a period tend toward the equilibrated triplet of subject-verb-complement.

Word order in French is fairly rigid, and the imbalanced sentences I have singled out are solutions to the problem of varying patterns in successive sentences. Another one is the absolute noun or pronoun placed at the beginning of a sentence and caught up by a reprise pronoun in the normal position.

> L'angoisse que je venais d'éprouver, je pensais que Swann s'en serait bien moqué s'il avait lu ma lettre et en avait deviné le but; or, au contraire, comme je l'ai appris plus tard, une angoisse semblable fut le tourment de longues années de sa vie, et personne aussi bien que lui peut-être n'aurait pu me comprendre; lui, cette angoisse qu'il y a à sentir l'être qu'on aime dans un lieu de plaisir où l'on n'est pas, où l'on ne peut pas le rejoindre, c'est l'amour qui la lui a fait connaître, l'amour, auquel elle est en quelque sorte prédestinée, par lequel elle sera accaparée, spécialisée; mais quand, comme pour moi, elle est entrée en nous avant qu'il ait encore fait

son apparition dans notre vie, elle flotte en l'attendant, vague et libre, sans affectation déterminée, au service un jour d'un sentiment, le lendemain d'un autre, tantôt de la tendresse filiale ou de l'amitié pour un camarade [1:30].

[As for the agony through which I had just passed, I imagined that Swann would have laughed heartily at it if he had read my letter and had guessed its purpose; whereas, on the contrary, as I was to learn in due course, a similar anguish had been the bane of his life for many years, and no one perhaps could have understood my feelings at that moment so well as himself; to him that anguish which lies in knowing that the creature one adores is in some place of enjoyment where oneself is not and cannot follow—to him that anguish came through Love, to which it is in a sense predestined, by which it must be equipped and adapted; but when, as had befallen me, such an anguish possesses one's soul before Love has yet entered into one's life, then it must drift, awaiting Love's coming, vague and free, without precise attachment, at the disposal of one sentiment today, of another tomorrow, of filial piety or affection for a comrade.]

It would have been possible to write "quant à l'angoisse, quant à lui," but those forms are rather mechanical and fail to endow French with an equivalent to the English or German sentences with an initial direct or indirect object ("him I see"). The absolute noun or pronoun construction, a creation evidently of the spoken language, while occasionally used by Pascal, Saint-Simon, or Chateaubriand, is perhaps more frequent in Proust's prose than in anyone's before. Especially when doubled, as here, or coupled with an apposition ("l'amour, auquel . . . ") it produces great vividness of expression. The passage is rendered all the more brilliant by the unusual pronoun references ("elle flotte en l'attendant") and the oscillation between *A* and *B* and *A, B* patterns. We have here densely Proustian syntax, the elements of which, however, are to be encountered in many less memorable places in *À la recherche*.

The opposite of the reprise pronoun is the anticipatory one, which, with its apposition, creates equally
asymmetrical effects.

> Que nous l'aimons—comme en ce moment j'aimais
> Françoise—, l'intermédiaire bien intentionné qui d'un mot
> vient de nous rendre supportable, humaine et presque pro-
> pice la fête inconcevable, infernale, au sein de laquelle nous
> croyions que des tourbillons ennemis, pervers et délicieux
> entraînaient loin de nous, la faisant rire de nous, celle que
> nous aimons! Si nous en jugeons par lui, le parent qui nous a
> accosté et qui est lui aussi un des inités des cruels mystères,
> les autres invités ne doivent rien avoir de bien démoniaque.
> Ces heures inaccessibles et suppliciantes où elle allait goûter
> des plaisirs inconnus, voici que par une brèche inespérée
> nous y pénétrons; voici qu'un des moments dont la succes-
> sion les aurait composées, un moment aussi réel que les
> autres, même peut-être plus important pour nous, parce que
> notre maîtresse y est plus mêlée, nous nous le représentons,
> nous le possédons, nous y intervenons, nous l'avons créé
> presque: le moment où on va lui dire que nous sommes là, en
> bas [1:31].

> [How we love him—as at that moment I loved Françoise—
> the good-natured intermediary who by a single word has
> made supportable, human, almost propitious the incon-
> ceivable, infernal scene of gaiety in the thick of which we had
> been imagining swarms of enemies, perverse and seductive,
> beguiling away from us, even making laugh at us, the
> woman whom we love. If we are to judge of them by him,
> this relative who has accosted us and who is himself an
> initiate in those cruel mysteries, then the other guests cannot
> be so very demoniacal. Those inaccessible and torturing
> hours into which she had gone to taste of unknown pleas-
> ures—behold, one of the moments whose series will go to
> make up their sum, a moment as genuine as the rest, if not
> actually more important to ourself because our mistress is
> more intensely a part of it; we picture it to ourselves, we
> possess it, we intervene upon it, almost we have created it:
> namely, the moment in which he goes to tell her that we are
> waiting there below.]

In the first of these sentences the apposition makes for

a great flowing complement after the brief initial subject and main verb; at the same time, the essential
words of the complement, "celle que nous aimons,"
are strikingly postponed, so that in one sentence we
find devices of tension and of relatively relaxed
movement—apposition normally being one of the
loosest, most casual syntactic connections. In the second sentence the binary pattern of "if" clause and
conclusion is made rhythmically tripartite by the apposition. Tension through to the end point returns in
the third main clause, with an impressive absolute
noun construction and final verb ("pénétrons"). The
structure of the long final sentence is so unusual as to
make one hesitate over the terminology for its description; the sequence might be characterized as absolute
noun, apposition to absolute noun, verbs with reprise
object, and apposition to the reprise pronoun, making
it then function as an anticipatory one. The four verbs
in asyndeton, with their multiple pauses, provide a
strikingly different rhythmic pattern for the center of
the sentence. Not a line in this wonderful passage is
conventional in structure; at the same time, every element belongs to real, living French. The only literary
constructions are the asyndetic juxtapositions and the
series of verbs, but these are old, essential parts of the
written language and its effects.

Asyndeton can range in function from being a
formal variation in aligning parallel words to a device
implying diffidence, hesitation, understated emphasis, and so forth. When it is constructed in twos—*A,
B*—the effect is usually one of asymmetry, but the best
test of the values of asyndeton is to repeat the phrase
or sentence, supplying "and" or "or" in the ordinary
places. The following passage would lose greatly by
being subjected to this test.

Puis il ne pouvait penser sans une grande lassitude que le lendemain il faudrait recommencer de chercher à savoir ce qu'Odette avait fait, à mettre en jeu des influences pour tâcher de la voir. Cette nécessité d'une activité sans trève, sans variété, sans résultats, lui était si cruelle qu'un jour, apercevant une grosseur sur son ventre, il ressentit une véritable joie à la pensée qu'il avait peut-être une tumeur mortelle, qu'il n'allait plus avoir à s'occuper de rien, que c'était la maladie qui allait le gouverner, faire de lui son jouet, jusqu'à la fin prochaine [1:317].

[After which he could not save himself from utter exhaustion at the thought that, next day, he must begin afresh his attempt to find out what Odette had been doing, must use all his influence to contrive to see her. This compulsion to an activity without respite, without variety, without result, was so cruel a scourge that one day, noticing a swelling over his stomach, he felt an actual joy in the idea that he had, perhaps, a tumor which would prove fatal, that he need not concern himself with anything further, that it was his malady which was going to govern his life, to make a plaything of him, until the not-distant end.]

Clearly asyndeton here represents the developing thought process; it is one of Proust's ways of indicating mental movement, as distinguished from formed thoughts cast in the normal syntactic mold. I should note as well that the *A, B, C* asyndeton is assimilated to the *A, B* kind in this passage. In isolation they can be separately classified, *A, B, C* being an old latinate pattern much used over the centuries, while *A, B* is uncommon in Latin (which uses *A, B-que* as alternative form) and has only a precarious existence outside relatively modern writers. Proust is certainly the greatest user of it in all its nuances, and one would not exaggerate in calling it the figure of the strongest asymmetry, just as *A* and *B* conveys stately equilibrium to a greater degree than any other device.

Polysyndeton is much rarer than asyndeton. Like asyndeton, the pattern of multiple coordination (*A* and

B and *C*) seems to have some basis in spoken style and sometimes is used to render familiar speech in fiction and plays. However, it also serves as a very formal and emphatic figure in poetry and elevated prose. Proust occasionally draws on it as in the following example, where the figure stands in sharp contrast to the preceding asyndeton.

> Et comme dans ce jeu où les Japonais s'amusent à tremper dans un bol de porcelaine rempli d'eau, de petits morceaux de papier jusque-là indistincts qui, à peine y sont-ils plongés, s'étirent, se contournent, se colorent, se différencient, deviennent des fleurs, des maisons, des personnages consistants et reconnaissables, de même maintenant toutes les fleurs de notre jardin et celles du parc de M. Swann, et les nymphéas de la Vivonne, et les bonnes gens du village et leurs petits logis et l'église et tout Combray et ses environs, tout cela qui prend forme et solidité, est sorti, ville et jardins, de ma tasse de thé [1:47–48].

> [And just as the Japanese amuse themselves by filling a porcelain bowl with water and steeping in it little bits of paper which until then are without character or form, but, the moment they become wet, stretch themselves and bend, take on color and distinctive shape, become flowers or houses or people, permanent and recognizable, so in that moment all the flowers in our garden and in M. Swann's park, and the waterlilies on the Vivonne and the good folk of the village and the whole of Combray and of its surroundings, taking their proper shape and growing solid, sprang into being, town and gardens alike, from my cup of tea.]

Polysyndeton is asymmetric or symmetrical, depending on the number of elements and length. *A* and *B* and *C* and *D* would normally tend to be equilibrated, but the eight nouns here are not only more numerous than is usual, but are subtly and asymmetrically grouped; *ville et jardins*, which summarizes them, is reinforced by another doubling (*forme et solidité*), so as to confer a stately end to this intricate period, which, of course, closes a chapter. The asyndeton earlier in the passage also deserves attention: the pattern made by verbs and complements (*A, B, C, D, E1, 2, 3*) belongs to a relatively old, if rare, type of arrangement in artistic French prose, to be found, for example, in La Bruyère's style or in Chateaubriand's prologue to *Atala*.

I have once had occasion to comment on elliptical syntax in Proust's prose. There is a slight distinction, not always easily made, between ellipsis and anacoluthon, the expressive disregard for grammatical consistency. In any case, asymmetry is the result.

> Un petit coup au carreau, comme si quelque chose l'avait heurté, suivi d'une ample chute légère comme de grains de sable qu'on eût laissés tomber d'une fenêtre au-dessus, puis la chute s'étendant, se réglant, adoptant un rhythme, devenant fluide, sonore, musicale, innombrable, universelle: c'était la pluie [1:101–2].

> [A little tap at the window, as though some missile had struck it, followed by a plentiful, falling sound, as light, though, as if a shower of sand were being sprinkled from a window overhead; then the fall spread, took on an order, a rhythm, became liquid, loud, drumming, musical, innumerable, universal. It was the rain.]

We recognize familiar elements here: the displacement of the main finite verb to near the end and the irregular combination of verbs and complements in asyndeton, *A, B, C1, D1, 2, 3, 4, 5*. But the truly remarkable thing is the heavily nominal character of the sentence, created partly by the very free handling of the present participle, used much as in English (which Scott Moncrieff, however, did not feel up to doing in his translation). Nominal syntax is rare in Proust's novel and quite expressive when it does occur; "se tenaient," the weak main verb of the passage quoted earlier about the staircase and domestic staff, creates a semantically nominal sentence, as does the mere "c'était" here. Proust generally avoids the verbless independent phrase, but we shall see at least one more example of a version of the nominal sentence.

In the passage on the rain, the series of participles and adjectival complements demonstrates the great ostentation nominal areas of the sentence can assume, which is sometimes another way of unbalancing the structure by focusing attention largely on one of its parts. In this stylistic domain we encounter the unexpected junctures of nouns and adjectives which are so characteristic of Proust's style; these unusual combinations are called "convergences" by Yvette Louria in her study, *La Convergeance stylistique chez Proust* (Geneva: Droz, 1957). The "escalier pestilentiel et désiré," with its false symmetry, is an example, and a more famous one is the description of the new matter he will use in describing dinners at Rivebelle: "Une matière distincte, nouvelle, d'une transparence, d'une sonorité spéciales, compacte, fraîchissante et rose" (3:871). The rare agreement of adjectives for the eye only and the peculiar sequence are both, of course, asymmetrical, but the very idea of such a conjunction of epithets also tends toward imbalance and weighting one part of a sentence at the expense of others. The traditional equilibrium of subject, verb, and complement implies, beyond syntax, some even distribution of semantic functions.

Whether one part of an asymmetrical sentence weakens another must be judged on the individual combination of semantics and syntax. Sometimes when the latter is periodic, emphasis is not distributed evenly, as in the following sentence, with its violent and expressive anacoluthon.

> Alors je m'aperçus qu'il y avait dans cette chambre un oeil-
> de-boeuf . . . et là, enchaîné sur un lit comme Prométhée
> sur son rocher, recevant les coups d'un martinet, en effet
> planté de clous que lui infligeait Maurice, je vis, déjà tout en
> sang, et couvert d'ecchymoses qui prouvaient que le sup-
> plice n'avait pas lieu pour la première fois, je vis devant moi
> M. de Charlus [3:815].

> [Then I noticed that this room had a small, round win-
> dow . . . and there, chained to a bed like Prometheus to his
> rock, and being beaten by Maurice with a cat-o'-nine tails
> which was, as a matter of fact, studded with nails, I saw
> before me M. de Charlus, bleeding all over and covered with
> welts which showed that this was not the first time the
> torture had taken place.]

Pascal was another inventor of styles who did not recoil from rejecting grammar for brilliance as Proust does here, when he makes "enchaîné" modify "M. de Charlus" and not "je," as it must in normal French prose. This particular irregularity of agreement gives the sentence an even more Latin air than does the postponed verb. The theory of the period, as European humanists derived it from Latin practice, involves opening a series of syntactic suspensions like the one beginning with "enchaîné," reinforced by "recevant," and making a complete picture with "couvert"; the suspensions (each participle equals a subordinate clause in Latin or French) are brought to what is imagistically a conclusion but lacks the one word the main clause must supply: "Charlus." Thus the period or "circle" consists of moving away from the chief grammatical line ("je m'aperçus") through subordinates; they, however, must lead back into the principal construction, whose completion cannot precede that of the subordinates. Only certain types of sentences can be made on this pattern in French, obviously. Proust was a master of the pattern, but the opposite, long sentences with additive syntax and no suspensions, also plays a role in his style. Having seen his version of the period, we must now look at the other extreme of sentence movement.

While a period may be irregular or asymmetrical in French because of the postposition of the verb, the effect is not so remote from the mainstream of stylistic practice as the additive sentence structure at its most elaborate. (Its simple form is merely a series of parallel relative clauses, varied perhaps with appositions, and somewhat reminiscent of the more monotonous forms of seventeenth-century prose style. See, for example, 1:54: "Ma tante se résignait . . . "). An additive sentence conceivably could be interrupted at many points; it generates no syntactic forward thrust, but is based on a semantic esthetic like the catalogues in many modern poems.

> C'étaient de ces chambres de province qui—de même qu'en certains pays des parties entières de l'air ou de la mer sont illuminées ou parfumées par des myriades de protozoaires que nous ne voyons pas—nous enchantent des mille odeurs qu'y dégagent les vertus, la sagesse, les habitudes, toute une vie secrète, invisible, surabondante et morale que l'atmosphère y tient en suspens; odeurs naturelles encore, certes, et couleur du temps comme celles de la campagne voisine, mais déjà casanières, humaines et renfermées, gelée exquise, industrieuse et limpide de tous les fruits de l'année qui ont quitté le verger pour l'armoire; saisonnières, mais mobilières et domestiques, corrigeant le piquant de la gelée blanche par la douceur du pain chaud, oisives et ponctuelles comme une horloge de village, flâneuses et rangées, insoucieuses et prévoyantes, lingères, matinales, dévotes, heureuses d'une paix qui n'apporte qu'un surcroit d'anxiété et d'un prosaïsme qui sert de grand réservoir de poésie à celui qui les traverse sans y avoir vécu [1:49].

> [They were rooms of that country order which (just as in certain climes whole tracts of air or ocean are illuminated or

scented by myriads of protozoa which we cannot see) fascinate our sense of smell with the countless odors springing
from their own special virtues, wisdom, habits, a whole
secret system of life, invisible, superabundant and profoundly moral, which their atmosphere holds in solution;
smells natural enough indeed, and colored by circumstances
as are those of the neighboring countryside, but already
humanized, domesticated, confined, an exquisite, skillful,
limpid jelly, blending all the fruits of the season which have
left the orchard for the storeroom, smells changing with the
year, but plenishing, domestic smells, which compensate for
the sharpness of hoar frost with the sweet savor of warm
bread, smells lazy and punctual as a village clock, roving
smells, pious smells; rejoicing in a peace which brings only
an increase of anxiety, and in a prosiness which serves as a
deep source of poetry to the stranger who passes through
their midst without having lived amongst them.]

In this passage the line usually drawn between
adjectives and substantives is especially weak, with a
remarkable effect of floating, indeterminate grammar.
Although syntactically there is no movement, the in-
teraction of the unusual adjoining terms creates a kind
of semantic excitement. With such mild and infrequent
verbs, the impression is predominantly of nominal
syntax, but interestingly enough, Proust is not much
tempted by the numerous mannerisms of the new
nominal tendencies of late nineteenth-century art
prose—verbal nouns in the plural, terms from the
painter's atelier, neuter substantivized adjectives, ex-
cessively long sequences of prepositional phrases, and
so forth. (The pastiche of the Goncourt journal in *Le
Temps retrouvé* shows Proust's great familiarity with
the style.) This kind of additive, nominal style, which
is necessarily asymmetric, lacking points of balance, is
much less common in Proust's prose than hypotaxis.
Actually, Proust is on the whole very much given to
verbs, as the elaborate adverbial material in his sen-

tences implies. Indeed, he shows at times a most peculiar taste for verbs.

> Quand j'aimais Albertine, je m'étais bien rendu compte qu'elle ne m'aimait pas, et j'avais été obligé de me résigner à ce qu'elle me fit seulement connaître ce que c'est qu'éprouver de la souffrance, de l'amour, et même au commencement, du bonheur [3:901–2].

> [When I was in love with Albertine, I realized clearly that she did not love me and I was forced to reconcile myself to merely learning from her what it is to experience suffering, love, and, at first, even happiness.]

Many writers would have phrased this more nominally: "compte de son indifférence à mon égard . . . étais résigné, par nécessité, à n'apprendre de mon amour que les sentiments de la souffrance." The verb-dominated sentence also lacks the strong subject-verb-complement articulation upon which our feelings of symmetry depend.

There is another, more frequent, kind of additive style than that composed of appositions of adjectives and nouns or parallel relative clauses.

> De ma chambre, je ne pouvais apercevoir que sa base [celle du clocher] qui avait été recouverte d'ardoises; mais quand, le dimanche, je les voyais, par une chaude matinée d'été flamboyer comme un soleil noir, je me disais: "Mon Dieu! neuf heures! il faut se préparer pour aller à la grand'messe si je veux avoir le temps d'aller embrasser tante Léonie avant", et je savais exactement la couleur qu'avait le soleil sur la place, la chaleur et la poussière du marché, l'ombre que faisait le store du magasin où maman entrerait peut-être avant la messe, dans une odeur de toile écrue, faire emplette de quelque mouchoir que lui ferait montrer, en cambrant la taille, le patron qui, tout en se préparant à fermer, venait d'aller dans l'arrière-boutique passer sa veste du dimanche et se savonner les mains qu'il avait l'habitude, toutes les cinq minutes, même dans les circonstances les plus mélancoliques, de frotter l'une contre l'autre d'un air d'entreprise, de partie fine et de réussite [1:64–65].

[From my bedroom window I could discern no more than the steeple's base, which had been freshly covered with slates; but when on Sundays I saw these, in the hot light of a summer morning, blaze like a black sun I would say to myself: "Good heavens! nine o'clock! I must get ready for mass at once if I am to have time to go in and kiss aunt Léonie first," and I would know exactly what was the color of the sunlight upon the Square, I could feel the heat and dust of the market, the shade behind the blinds of the shop into which Mama would perhaps go on her way to mass, penetrating its odor of unbleached calico, to purchase a handkerchief or something, of which the draper himself would let her see what he had, bowing from the waist: who, having made everything ready for shutting up, had just gone into the back shop to put on his Sunday coat and to wash his hands, which it was his habit, every few minutes and even on the saddest occasions, to rub one against the other with an air of enterprise, cunning, and success.]

Here the concatenation of subordinate clauses, each one depending on the preceding one, moves completely away from the main clause and spectacularly violates the general periodic conception of the necessary logical relations between independent clause and relatives. The asymmetry is one of both sense and syntax.

This enchained form of additive hypotaxis brings us to some basic questions about Proust's style. Except for one or two essayistic passages on love, examples of it tend to describe intermittent, momentary feelings or impressions. They are the material of which other novelists might make interior monologue. There are theoretical reasons, however, why Proust does not use interior monologue: that we can only fully grasp what is past, absent, means that the stream of consciousness does not really contain the whole of experience; the broken phrases and notations, which are supposed to be consciousness itself, either pretend to take in more than we are aware of perceiving in reality or show how inferior conscious perceptions are. The various contentions about whether we always think with words and at what point syntax enters into our thoughts indicates how uneasy we feel about conveying the shifting content of our minds in writing. (A résumé of discussions of these problems can be found in Dorrit Cohn's *Transparent Minds: Narrative Modes for Presenting Consciousness in Fiction* [Princeton, N. J.: Princeton University Press, 1978], pp. 77–80.) Proust's theory is that just as experience must be passed through the faculty of memory to be apprehended in all its significant detail, so the putting of it into language involves not some raw pseudorepresentation of it, but the "translation" of impressions into the medium of art. There ordering syntax and often hypotaxis, the conventions of art, will obtain. We might compare a passage from a familiar "imagist" poem with its recreation in hypotactic prose.

> The winter evening settles down
> With smell of steaks in passageways.
> Six o'clock.
> The burnt-out ends of smoky days.
> And now a gusty shower wraps
> The grimy scraps
> Of withered leaves about your feet
> And newspapers from vacant lots;
> The showers beat
> On broken blinds and chimney-pots,
> And at the corner of the street
> A lonely cab-horse steams and stamps
> And then the lighting of the lamps.

The heavy use of "and," the address to oneself, and the sentence fragments are characteristic of stream-of-consciousness writing.

> When, at six o'clock, the winter evening settles down—
> resembling the burnt-out end of a smoky day—as the smell

of steak rises in passageways, I feel around my feet the scraps
of withered leaves, driven by the gusty shower, as well as
newspapers from vacant lots, where the reverberation of the
shower echoes from broken blinds and chimney pots, while,
at the corner of the street, during the lighting of the lamps, a
lonely cab-horse steams and stamps.

The superiority of Eliot's "Preludes I" over its "translation" should not blind us to the qualities peculiar to
the prose. Instead of the nihilistic feeling, of being
able to connect nothing with nothing, which is so
typical of American modernism, the hypotactic prose
version gives the impression of being a preparation
for some significant thought or event. The elaborate
syntax—including Proust's favorite double initial
adverbial clause—implies an active, ordering, not in
the least weary intelligence. The tone is less bleak,
more melancholy.

It is not solely the influence of the highly intel-
lectualized French tradition of novelistic texture that
inclines Proust toward hypotactic descriptions. When
the narrator perceives a beautiful landscape, he is making a conscious effort, as with experiences of involuntary memory, to seize the nature of that beauty, and
syntactic elaboration conveys the process. His descriptions, which of course are illuminated by the retro-
spective vision of art, are rendered with great detail
and awareness, as befits the special state of mind of
esthetic contemplation, which, although not desig-
nated by any particular psychological term, is a
strongly implicit concept in Proust's novel. In esthetic
contemplation, the tension between subject and object
disappears, the landscape momentarily ceasing to be
the unseizable thing-in-itself. Often the descriptions
are interpretive.

Il faisait une nuit transparente et sans un souffle;
j'imaginais que la Seine coulant entre ses ponts circulaires,

faits de leur plateau et de son reflet, devait ressembler au Bosphore. Et, symbole soit de cette invasion que prédisait le défaitisme de M. de Charlus, soit de la coopération de nos frères musulmans avec les armées de la France, la lune étroite et recourbée comme un sequin semblait mettre le ciel parisien sous le signe oriental du croissant [3:808–9].

[It was a transparently clear night, without a breath of air stirring. I imagined that the Seine, flowing through the hoops formed by the bridges and the reflection of their arches in the water, must resemble the Bosporus. And as a symbol either of the invasion prophecied by M. de Charlus's defeatism, or of the cooperation of our Moslem brothers with the armies of France, the slender, curved moon, recalling a sequin, seemed to place the Parisian sky under the Oriental sign of the crescent.]

What we do not have in Proust's novel is the solipsistic, dreamy state of mind, the confusion of inner and outer, so characteristic of modern fiction. The landscapes are not moods in the ordinary sense. As a consequence, there is little significant recurring imagery, no symbols of which the narrator is only half aware. When he sees something, he really looks at it with all his attention. (It is not surprising, therefore, that he sees little when the age of myth is over at the end of *À l'ombre* and the beginning of *Le Côté de Guermantes;* most of the major descriptions are clustered early in *À la recherche.*)

There are rare exceptions to Proust's usual manner of describing. One occurs in the passage, written in rather plain sentences, where the narrator realizes the gravity of his grandmother's condition (she has just had a stroke).

Le professeur tempêtait toujours pendant que je regardais sur le palier ma grand'mère qui était perdue. Chaque personne est bien seul. Nous repartîmes vers la maison.
Le soleil déclinait; il enflammait un interminable mur

que notre fiacre avait à longer avant d'arriver à la rue que
nous habitions, mur sur lequel l'ombre, projetée par le
couchant, du cheval et de la voiture, se détachait en noir sur
le fond rougeâtre, comme un char funèbre dans une terre
cuite de Pompéi. Enfin nous arrivâmes [2:318].

[The Professor continued to storm while I stood on the land-
ing gazing at a grandmother for whom there was not the
slightest hope. Each of us is indeed alone. We started for
home.
      The sun was sinking, it burnished an interminable wall
along which our cab had to pass before reaching the street in
which we lived, a wall against which the shadow cast by the
setting sun of horse and carriage stood out in black on a
ruddy background, like a funeral car on some Pompeian
terra cotta. At length we arrived at the house.]

This kind of background imagery is what we find in
such lyrical novels of the 1920s as *The Waves, Thérèse
Desqueyroux,* or *A Farewell to Arms.* It involves exactly
that half awareness of the surroundings that charac-
terizes the symbolic descriptions commonly found in
fiction more or less contemporary with Proust's; it
represents subliminal perception and mood imagery,
which are the exception in *À la recherche.*

Besides description, hypotaxis has some other
obviously valuable functions for Proust. The narrator's
neurotic, involved, and contradictory reactions depend on elaborate principles of cause and effect which
are nicely rendered by subordination. Cause and effect
are also the underlying principles for the presentation
of much of the social comedy of the novel, as in the
long excursus during the duchess of Guermantes's
dinner party. Furthermore, social values, in the absence of an "activité sociale véritable" (2:470), are
largely verbal creations, devised by talk and subject to
demolition by such brilliant discussion as Proust's.
Hypotaxis not only can make logical rapprochements,

but also can represent an idea of several parts, such as would be difficult to present with simultaneity in stream-of-consciousness writing. Glancing at an invitation, the narrator thinks:

> Et certes il y a seulement deux jours, si fatigué de vie mondaine que je fusse, c'eût été un vrai plaisir pour moi que de la goûter transplantée dans ces jardins où poussaient en pleine terre, grâce à l'exposition de Féterne, les figuiers, les palmiers, les plants de rosiers, jusque dans la mer souvent d'un calme et d'un bleu méditerranéens et sur laquelle le petit yacht des propriétaires allait, avant le commencement de la fête, chercher, dans les plages de l'autre côté de la baie, les invités les plus importants, servait, avec ses velums tendus contre le soleil, quand tout le monde était arrivé, de salle à manger pour goûter, et repartait le soir reconduire ceux qu'il avait amenés [2:767].

> [To be sure, as recently as the day before yesterday, tired as I was of the social round, it would have been a real pleasure to me to taste it, transplanted amid those gardens in which there grew in the open air, thanks to the exposure of Feterne, fig trees, palms, rose bushes extended down to a sea as blue and calm often as the Mediterranean, upon which the host's little yacht sped across, before the party began, to fetch from the places on the other side of the bay the most important guests, served, with its awnings spread to shut out the sun, after the party had assembled, as an open air refreshment room, and set sail again in the evening to take back those whom it had brought.]

The total course of the *matinée*, which momentarily flashes into the narrator's mind, is packed into one sentence, avoiding narrative. Hypotaxis can, in other words, serve as a stylized representation of complex simultaneity, which is, in the absolute sense, impossible to convey in literature. Again we see the appropriateness of Proust's idea that writing a novel is "translating," with all the conversions and adaptations that implies.

To return for a moment to our hypotactic point of departure, we see that the long sentence describing the look and heat of the square in Combray uses grammatical relations emptied of their logical content (the relative clause serves best for this purpose) to express unmeasurable degrees of associational and temporal movement. It is a compromise between the inherited conventions of literature and the acknowledgment that traditional syntax imperfectly indicates the nature of mental processes. But this compromise is not an unworthy resort; through art, intuition, and reflection, Proust is recreating what the mind really experiences rather than the dim, unsatisfying events of consciousness, which cannot seize the totality of what actually goes on. And as we reflect on this, it becomes evident that all the devices of asymmetry—asyndeton, additive structures, polysyndeton, radical hypotaxis, parenthesis, absolute nouns—are part of this recreation, which indeed reveals associative or indirect movement of the mind, but not the confusion or lack of focus that might often seem to be our mental condition. Proust has devised a syntax which describes the ideal processes of the mind, ones we can imagine but not seize in their actual workings, a synthesis of logical articulations and subordinating movements indicative of elliptic ramifications. It is, of course, no more stylized than the stream-of-consciousness technique, which becomes highly individual and conventionalized in the work of every novelist using it. Like the interior monologue, Proust's style originates in a probably unconscious reaction to the theories of the logic of grammar, which were elaborated during the Enlightenment and of which a famous example in French is the comte de Rivarol's *Discours*. For such theorists there was a "natural" word

order, which was the expression of reason and toward
which it was normal to incline. Even though we disbe-
lieve such notions, we still associate the regular
subject-verb-complement arrangement with rational
exposition, and subordinate clauses with fuller but
limited explanation or with restrictive qualifications.
Proust's style constitutes one vast allusion to the theory of natural, logical syntax, demonstrating as it does
that the mind often naturally proceeds in the equivalent of an irregular, asymmetrical discourse, in which
tools like hypotaxis serve unpredictable functions.

While the verbless fragment is rare in Proust and
the tendency toward hypotaxis strong, at times
Proust, with much use of questions, even moves toward something like an interior monologue without
ever quite going so far (3:84, 151, 340, 346, 422, 474).
These passages are concentrated in *La Prisonnière* and
La Fugitive, where, furthermore, we are especially
aware that the narrator is experiencing violent oscil-
lations between actual feelings and what he thinks he
should feel. Expressions such as "I felt that" or "I did
not know that" sometimes make us perceive temporal
levels; at other times we simply notice the narrator
shifting in sentence after sentence from one perspective to another. While the tenses do not necessarily
reveal it, the narrator's mind moves suddenly from
one point in time to another, and we become especially
conscious of these *anachronies*, as Gérard Genette calls
them, which, though present in many places in *À la
recherche*, especially force themselves upon the attention here. (For Genette's discussion of *anachronies* see
Figures III [Paris: Seuil, 1972], pp. 79–89.) Of course,
Proust's contention that the *I* is a "series of events,"
rather than a stable organism, should lead precisely to
syntax adjusted to render unexpected rapproche-

ments and lapses into discontinuity. But for illustrations of the larger picture of mental movement, we must look to the sequentiality of sentences.

There is a wonderful example of indirection on the first page of *Swann*. After numerous rather short, even paratactic sentences—it is not always remembered how simple the grammar of the opening passage is—the narrator forms a mental picture that is richer than what would seem motivated.

> . . . j'entendais le sifflement des trains qui, plus ou moins éloigné, comme le chant d'un oiseau dans une forêt, relevant les distances, me décrivait l'étendue de la campagne déserte où le voyageur se hâte vers la station prochaine; et le petit chemin qu'il suit va être gravé dans son souvenir par l'excitation qu'il doit à des lieux nouveaux, à des actes inaccoutumés, à la causerie récente et aux adieux sous la lampe étrangère qui le suivent encore dans le silence de la nuit, à la douceur prochaine du retour [1:3–4].

> [. . . I could hear the whistling of trains, which, now nearer and now farther off, punctuating the distance like the note of a bird in a forest, showed me in perspective the deserted countryside through which a traveller would be hurrying towards the nearest station: the path that he followed being fixed forever in his memory by the general excitement due to being in a strange place, to doing unusual things, to the last words of conversation, to farewells exchanged beneath an unfamiliar lamp which echoed still in his ears amid the silence of the night; and to the delightful prospect of being once again at home.]

The "et" after the semicolon has almost the force of "de sorte que"; there is no true parallelism at all between the two independent clauses, and the "et" is the one of movement Proust so admired in Flaubert. The "il" referring to a noun in a doubly subordinate clause represents not only a peculiar grammatical sequence (that is, reference to a completely incidental noun), but is also an extraordinary example of continuity, again of the type Proust admired in Flaubert's work. The stunning asymmetries of the concluding prepositional phrases represent such a unique combination of variables that doubtless no other writer had ever devised its like: $A(\grave{a})$, $B(\grave{a})$, $C(\grave{a})$ *et* $D(aux)$, $E(\grave{a})$. The total effect is one of gentle expansion, beginning with "et le petit chemin" and continuing with ever more unpredictable details; solidly symmetrical prose would be too emphatic, too obviously disconnected with what precedes, for indefinite pauses and movement are a particular trait of much asymmetrical prose, and closure with a solid cadence, as in the *A* and *B* formula, belongs especially to regular, balancing prose.

Continuity by pronoun reference to subordinate and twice subordinate clauses occurs in other places.

> . . . on s'étonnait même que Françoise lui laissât faire tant de courses et de besogne, car elle commençait à porter difficilement devant elle la mystérieuse corbeille, chaque jour plus remplie, dont on devinait sous ses amples sarraux la forme magnifique. Ceux-ci rappelaient les houppelandes qui revêtent certaines des figures symbolique de Giotto dont M. Swann m'avait donné des photographies. C'est lui-même qui nous l'avait fait remarquer et quand il nous demandait des nouvelles de la fille de cuisine, il nous disait: "Comment va la Charité de Giotto?" [1:80].

> [. . . it was indeed surprising that Françoise allowed her to run so many errands in the town and to do so much work in the house, for she was beginning to find difficulty in bearing before her the mysterious casket, fuller and larger every day, whose splendid outline could be detected through the folds of her ample smocks. These last recalled the cloaks in which Giotto shrouds some of the allegorical figures in his paintings, of which M. Swann had given me photographs. He it was who pointed out the resemblance, and when he inquired after the kitchen-maid he would say: "Well, how goes it with Giotto's Charity?"]

Here, as elsewhere, Proust violates conventions of

prose discourse which are more implicit in traditional practice than expressly stated in grammatical treatises.

The next example is even more surprising.

> Le brouillard lui-même par les clartés confortables de l'intérieur [du restaurant], semblait jusque sur le trottoir vous indiquer l'entrée avec la joie de ces valets qui reflètent les dispositions du maître; il s'irisait des nuances les plus délicates et montrait l'entrée comme la colonne lumineuse qui guida les Hébreux. Il y en avait d'ailleurs beaucoup dans la clientèle [2:400].

> [The fog itself, beside the comfortable brightness of the lighted interior of the restaurant, seemed to be waiting outside on the pavement to show one the way in with the joy of servants whose faces reflect the hospitable instincts of the master; shot with the most delicate shades of light, it pointed the way like the pillar of fire which guided the Children of Israel. Many of whom, as it happened, were to be found inside.]

What is most impressive, perhaps, about Proust's achievement here is his finding a grammatical solution for problems in the representation of thought where lesser writers would have resorted to a purely descriptive, periphrastic one: *cela me fit penser que, cela me rappela*. When he praised Flaubert above all as a creator of syntax, almost equaling in originality Kant with his categories and *Critiques*, Proust revealed his utmost concern with just such details as these.

Finally, there are many shifts in focus in *À la recherche* which depend on references to what precedes, without taking so precisely original a grammatical pattern. In the following passage the narrator, who has been talking about how a hotel employee refers to the chauffeur as a "monsieur," is mentioning the rigid "Combray" ideas of caste his mother retains.

> Elle eût donné aussi difficilement la main à un valet de

chambre qu'elle lui donnait aisément dix francs (lesquels lui
faisaient, du reste, beaucoup plus de plaisir). Pour elle,
qu'elle l'avouât ou non, les maîtres étaient les maîtres et les
domestiques étaient les gens qui mangeaient à la cuisine.
Quand elle voyait un chauffeur d'automobile dîner avec moi
dans la salle à manger, elle n'était pas absolument contente et
me disait: "Il me semble que tu pourrais avoir mieux comme
ami qu'un mécanicien", comme elle aurait dit, s'il se fût agi
de mariage: "Tu pourrais trouver mieux comme parti." Le
chauffeur (heureusement je ne songeai jamais à inviter celui-
là) était venu me dire que la Compagnie . . . lui faisait re-
joindre Paris dès le lendemain [2:102–7].

[She would have been as reluctant to give her hand to a
footman as she would have been ready to give him ten francs
(which for that matter he was far more glad to receive). To
her, whether she admitted it or not, masters were masters,
and servants were the people who fed in the kitchen. When
she saw the driver of a motor car dining with me in the
restaurant, she was not altogether pleased, and said to me:
"It seems to me you might have a more suitable friend than a
mechanic," as she might have said, had it been a question of
my marriage: "You might find somebody better than that."
This particular chauffeur (fortunately I never dreamed of
inviting him to dinner) had come to tell me that the company
had ordered him to return to Paris on the following day.]

Here a hypothetical chauffeur, brought in as illustration, unexpectedly leads us back to the real chauffeur
of whom the hotel employee had spoken. Since we
have never seen the narrator dine with a chauffeur,
hypothetical or otherwise, the narrator's train of
thought seems especially indirect.

At the same time, however, as we observe associative movement in Proust's prose, we must remember that there is an interplay in his work between
logical sequence and indirection, just as there is between symmetry and asymmetry in sentence structure. Earlier I pointed out that in the descriptions of the
two "ways" in Combray, both appearing quite complicated on the surface, that of the Méséglise way is

actually organized in a relatively conventional temporal and geographic fashion, while that of the Guermantes way relies more on associationism. In much the same manner we can discover very neatly structured plans beneath such efflorescent detail as that describing the church portal and interior in Combray. In other places Proust's method is different. I have tended by and large in this chapter to talk of asymmetries and additive structures of an alogical nature, since therein lie the more obviously unusual aspects of Proust's style, and certainly Proust intended the reader to be immediately aware of them, for the first fifty pages of *Swann* contain an especially great number of irregular sentences. Noting this characteristic of *Swann* and remembering that the essayistic, maximlike material is most developed near the very end of the whole novel, we might take the idea of a *recherche*, an exploration and quest, with its share of inconclusiveness, false directions, and surprises, as the guiding principle of which Proust's style and thematic content are the varying facets, the one susceptible of grammatical analysis, the other of paraphrase.

On the simplest level, asyndeton tends to suggest a progression which is not concluded, which retains a certain tentative quality. Proust creates a similarly irregular effect by heterogeneity of material: "l'ivresse de l'orage, la puissance de l'hygiène, la stupidité de mon éducation, et la symétrie des jardins." Neither type of expression gives the impression of a logically worked out, terminated process, a preestablished classification and definitive system of thought. The asymmetrical sentence serves the same purpose, since it is opposed to the conception of neat writing, expressive of a plan and outline with which the writer has limited, defined, and regularized his thought before putting it into words. (Such is the classical theory of fine prose, as set forth by Buffon and used as the basis of the doctrine of writing taught in the lycée; the exercise called *dissertation française* might be called the most anti-Proustian mode of writing.)

Proust's narrator encounters phenomena which he is able to describe in terms of a process before their significance is clear, and thus we have expressions like "toutes les fleurs de notre jardin et celles du parc de M. Swann, et les nymphéas de la Vivonne, et ies bonnes gens du village et l'église et tout Combray et ses environs." He is seizing what is happening rather than summarizing it, for summary narration, so uncommon in Proust, reflects a distant, settled conception of things. It is rather the principle of profusion which is at work in Proust's prose. One also finds sentences with reprise or anticipatory pronouns, which are simply vast elaborations of the devious colloquial habit of thinking of a person or object, then working out what one has to say: "des chutes de neige pareilles on n'en a pas vu depuis bien longtemps." As for appositions, they supply what one cannot easily put into the sentence, for they represent one of the loosest grammatical joinings; the mind explores at the expense of tight syntax. The sentence with multiple elements, whether they consist of subordinate clauses yoking together things which have no immediate relevance to each other or of a series of more or less circumstantial expressions ("moi qui oublieux . . . reste là, devant le clocher, pendant des heures, immobile, essayant de me souvenir, sentant au fond de moi des terres reconquises"), renders the plentitude, heterogeneity, or logical discontinuity of experience before philosophical reflection has accounted for it.

It does not matter whether every sentence in

Proust which expresses irrational mental phenomena, paradoxes, temporal subjectivity, or a mysterious gap in reality actually has one of the irregular shapes I have described. Proust's prose forms an explorative discourse in which the general tendencies of the syntax color the whole and which functions often in extended passages, like the wonderful comparison between Aunt Léonie and Louis XIV (1:118–19). This latter passage, although using a number of the syntactic details I have examined, impresses the reader more by the gradual, almost insidious way one moves into the comparison than by specific grammatical devices. Thus the paradoxes and antinomies of *À la recherche* cannot always be isolated in a single sentence or even passage. Or, as Genette has demonstrated, *achronies* slip into the sentence without there being any necessarily peculiar stylistic expression of them.

The expository method I have followed in this book, beginning with the largest thematic outlines before moving into the details of expression, is exactly the opposite of Proust's discourse, where there is a concentration of generalities, retrospectively illuminating the novel, as the narrator meditates in the princess of Guermantes's library. There we find a succession of *idées claires* in the French tradition, but *idées claires* concerning impressions which are not at all clear and which bear no relation to the propagandistic simplicities of the usual novel of ideas, as represented by the works of Maurice Barrès or Paul Bourget.

The justification for our taking a short cut to the intellectual structure of the novel is simply that it demands more years of studying Proust than many readers have at their disposal to apprehend the wholeness of *À la recherche,* and even with much guidance and experience, there always remains a great deal to be discovered and reflected on. Proust's prose is so complex that I can imagine systems of analysis other than mine, which is essentially rhetorical and grammatical, that would illuminate its curious movement. However, it is clear that the devices of indirection and irregularity are there to serve as an experimental induction to a kind of thought which aspires to encompass the totality of experience. Such thought must authenticate itself by a lengthy demonstration in which there seem to be false conclusions, misleading indications, unexpected relationships, and a plenitude of ideas, feelings, and sensations that cannot be immediately accounted for.

conclusion

Proust's point of departure for an elaborate intellectual development of an idea—the unknowability of
the Other, for example—is often some commonplace
of experience. Others are indeed difficult to fathom
absolutely; the past is ambiguous in its reality, and we
are not governed always by purely reasonable mental
phemonena. What makes Proust's treatment of these
ordinary aspects of experience striking is his pushing
the idea of the Other or of the irrationality of involuntary memory to the point where it becomes a *problem*:
that is, it is elevated to a philosophical question. When
we see that the notion of the Other or our perception of
time is essentially strange even by ordinary rational
standards, we then see that the technique of the novel,
as it had been practiced before Proust rests on various
assumptions that suit our practical sense of reason but
are easily impaired by analysis. A novel is actually a
very peculiar thing, in that it gives us the impression
that we know characters with a kind of knowledge that

is impossible or makes us cover years of existence in a few hours; we accept conventions in fiction that are not founded on our experience of life. Proust chooses to reexamine the novel in terms of a higher or philosophical reason that destroys the neat catagories of time and individuality current before him. Again, his intellectual gesture is to scrutinize radically what we all know, that novels are not life, and in so doing, he arrives at another kind of novel, which questions the reliability of much of the narrator's experience. The criticism of reason in Proust's novel, as in the work of Kant before him, consists of turning rationality against itself, of rising to a higher, self-conscious form of reason. However, there is a world of difference between the abstract style of German philosophy and the mood of Proust's novel.

The perception of things in the realist novel before Proust, for all its attempts at particularization, seldom was truly individualized. Again, like the conception of characters or the handling of time, the rendering of sights and sounds was, almost by the very limitations of vocabulary, conventionalized. Proust therefore evolved a way of metaphorically—and thus more particularly—describing the concrete, and often even the abstract. However, we must not confuse his achievement with mere technique. Proust disliked the constant stream of metaphors in a writer like Gautier, for whom imagery was a kind of automatic, necessary embellishment that one learned to produce, like any other aspect of fine writing. Rather, Proust made an esthetic mystique of metaphor: if figurative language does not have an absolute authenticity, it is better not to use it, but when the metaphor is the right one, it gives a kind of eternity to style (3:889). We see here both the Symbolist insistence on figurative language and, in Proust's characterization of its effect, the parallel with Christian soteriology that marks his ethical thought.

Proust is the only artist besides Stéphane Mallarmé to have worked out carefully the implications of that use of religious terms for art which was commonplace in Symbolist circles and to have conceived of the salvation of art as more than a rather vague, high-toned expression. Furthermore, the cyclical thinking widespread in romantic and modern artists is more nearly identified in Proust's novel with the one-time cycle of Christian thought ("In my end is my beginning") than it is in the cyclical poetic designs of, say, Rimbaud. Proust's renunciation of life is also closer to the traditional Christian pattern of a reaction arising from experience, rather than to the unintentionally comic way Axël renounces life in Villiers de l'Isle-Adam's play, a gesture which is based on pure Symbolist theory, unsupported by any serious acquaintance with life outside Axël's castle.

Proust wisely discarded an early projected title for his novel, which was "L'Adoration perpétuelle," referring to a special worship of the Eucharist and redolent of cloisters, emotional vows, and Chateaubrianesque religiosity, whose perfervid tone tends to invite irreverent reflections. Actually, Proust's imagery in general does not follow the strain of romantic Catholicism, autumnal decadence, or the Symbolists' various expressions of pessimism: Odette's etiolated orchids-and-Botticelli days were not her best. There is a pronounced dominance of spring and summer landscapes in *À la recherche* and a distinct delight in urban luxury. Balancing the late nineteenth-century fondness for synesthesia and metaphors taken from the fine arts is an abundance of scientific and mechanical imagery;

the modernist side of Proust's taste is very noticable and is connected with the fact that he saw culture and society as moving through endless cycles, rather than reaching their definitive end in his own day. Thus we see that despite the highly pessimistic Schopenhauerian cast of much of his thought, the imagery which gives its tone to the novel differs distinctly from that of the decadent imagination, and, even in the realm of thought, pessimism recedes at a certain point as the narrator reflects that "l'oeuvre est signe de bonheur" (3:904); art is happiness in that its pleasures are intellectual and not bound to matter, which is the way of death. In other words, we find that the narrator has arrived in the end at the most curious paradox of all: he manages to do what Schopenhauer was unable to do, to derive a conception of happiness from the principles of pessimist idealism.

index